MW01536059

PEANUTS

2013 CALENDAR

Andrews McMeel Publishing, LLC

Kansas City • Sydney • London

Peanuts 2013 Calendar © 2011 by Peanuts Worldwide LLC. Printed in China.
No part of this calendar may be used or reproduced in any manner whatsoever without written permission except in the case of reprints in the context of reviews. For information write Andrews McMeel Publishing, LLC, an Andrews McMeel Universal company,
1130 Walnut Street, Kansas City, Missouri 64106.

www.andrewsmcmeel.com

ISBN-13: 978-1-4494-1949-3

2013

JANUARY

S	M	T	W	T	F	S
		1	2	3	4	5
6	7	8	9	10	11	12
13	14	15	16	17	18	19
20	21	22	23	24	25	26
27	28	29	30	31		

FEBRUARY

S	M	T	W	T	F	S
					1	2
3	4	5	6	7	8	9
10	11	12	13	14	15	16
17	18	19	20	21	22	23
24	25	26	27	28		

MARCH

S	M	T	W	T	F	S
					1	2
3	4	5	6	7	8	9
10	11	12	13	14	15	16
17	18	19	20	21	22	23
24	25	26	27	28	29	30
31						

APRIL

S	M	T	W	T	F	S
	1	2	3	4	5	6
7	8	9	10	11	12	13
14	15	16	17	18	19	20
21	22	23	24	25	26	27
28	29	30				

MAY

S	M	T	W	T	F	S
			1	2	3	4
5	6	7	8	9	10	11
12	13	14	15	16	17	18
19	20	21	22	23	24	25
26	27	28	29	30	31	

JUNE

S	M	T	W	T	F	S
						1
2	3	4	5	6	7	8
9	10	11	12	13	14	15
16	17	18	19	20	21	22
23	24	25	26	27	28	29
30						

JULY

S	M	T	W	T	F	S
	1	2	3	4	5	6
7	8	9	10	11	12	13
14	15	16	17	18	19	20
21	22	23	24	25	26	27
28	29	30	31			

AUGUST

S	M	T	W	T	F	S
				1	2	3
4	5	6	7	8	9	10
11	12	13	14	15	16	17
18	19	20	21	22	23	24
25	26	27	28	29	30	31

SEPTEMBER

S	M	T	W	T	F	S
1	2	3	4	5	6	7
8	9	10	11	12	13	14
15	16	17	18	19	20	21
22	23	24	25	26	27	28
29	30					

OCTOBER

S	M	T	W	T	F	S
		1	2	3	4	5
6	7	8	9	10	11	12
13	14	15	16	17	18	19
20	21	22	23	24	25	26
27	28	29	30	31		

NOVEMBER

S	M	T	W	T	F	S
					1	2
3	4	5	6	7	8	9
10	11	12	13	14	15	16
17	18	19	20	21	22	23
24	25	26	27	28	29	30

DECEMBER

S	M	T	W	T	F	S
1	2	3	4	5	6	7
8	9	10	11	12	13	14
15	16	17	18	19	20	21
22	23	24	25	26	27	28
29	30	31				

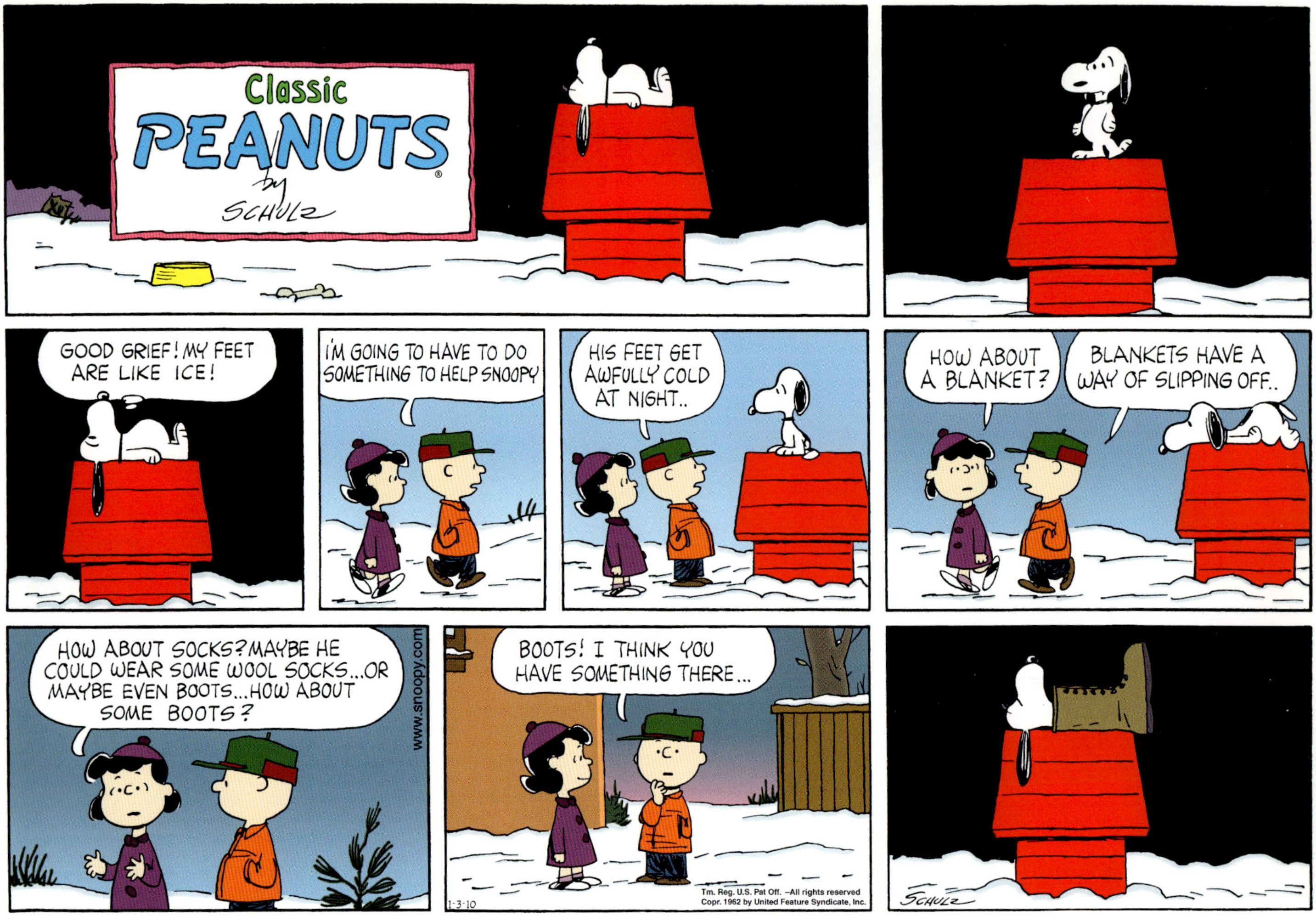
Classic
PEANUTS
by
SCHULZ
GOOD GRIEF! MY FEET ARE LIKE ICE!
I'M GOING TO HAVE TO DO SOMETHING TO HELP SNOOPY
HIS FEET GET AWFULLY COLD AT NIGHT..
HOW ABOUT A BLANKET?
BLANKETS HAVE A WAY OF SLIPPING OFF..
HOW ABOUT SOCKS? MAYBE HE COULD WEAR SOME WOOL SOCKS...OR MAYBE EVEN BOOTS...HOW ABOUT SOME BOOTS?
www.snoopy.com
BOOTS! I THINK YOU HAVE SOMETHING THERE...
1-3-10
Tm. Reg. U.S. Pat Off. –All rights reserved
Copr. 1962 by United Feature Syndicate, Inc.
SCHULZ

NOTES

December 2012

S	M	T	W	T	F	S
						1
2	3	4	5	6	7	8
9	10	11	12	13	14	15
16	17	18	19	20	21	22
23	24	25	26	27	28	29
30	31					

January 2013

S	M	T	W	T	F	S
		1	2	3	4	5
6	7	8	9	10	11	12
13	14	15	16	17	18	19
20	21	22	23	24	25	26
27	28	29	30	31		

DECEMBER 2012–JANUARY 2013

31 MONDAY

1 TUESDAY

New Year's Day

Kwanzaa ends (USA)

2 WEDNESDAY

New Year's Day (observed) (NZ)

Bank Holiday (UK—Scotland)

3 THURSDAY

4 FRIDAY

5 SATURDAY

6 SUNDAY

Classic
PEANUTS
by SCHULZ
I GET DIZZY THINKING ABOUT IT!
IT STAGGERS THE IMAGINATION...
JUST THINK..OUT OF THE BILLIONS AND BILLIONS OF SNOWFLAKES THAT HAVE FALLEN, NO TWO HAVE EVER BEEN ALIKE!
IT'S MAKES THE MIND REEL...
!
LUCY! LUCY! COME QUICK! I SAW THEM! I SAW THEM!
Tm. Reg. U.S. Pat Off.—All rights reserved
Copr. 1963 by United Feature Syndicate, Inc.
1-10-10
www.snoopy.com
I SAW TWO SNOWFLAKES THAT WERE **EXACTLY** ALIKE!! COME QUICK!
THAT'S FUNNY...THEY WERE AROUND HERE SOMEWHERE..
SCHULZ

NOTES

January 2013

S	M	T	W	T	F	S
		1	2	3	4	5
6	7	8	9	10	11	12
13	14	15	16	17	18	19
20	21	22	23	24	25	26
27	28	29	30	31		

JANUARY

7 MONDAY

8 TUESDAY

9 WEDNESDAY

10 THURSDAY

11 FRIDAY

12 SATURDAY

13 SUNDAY

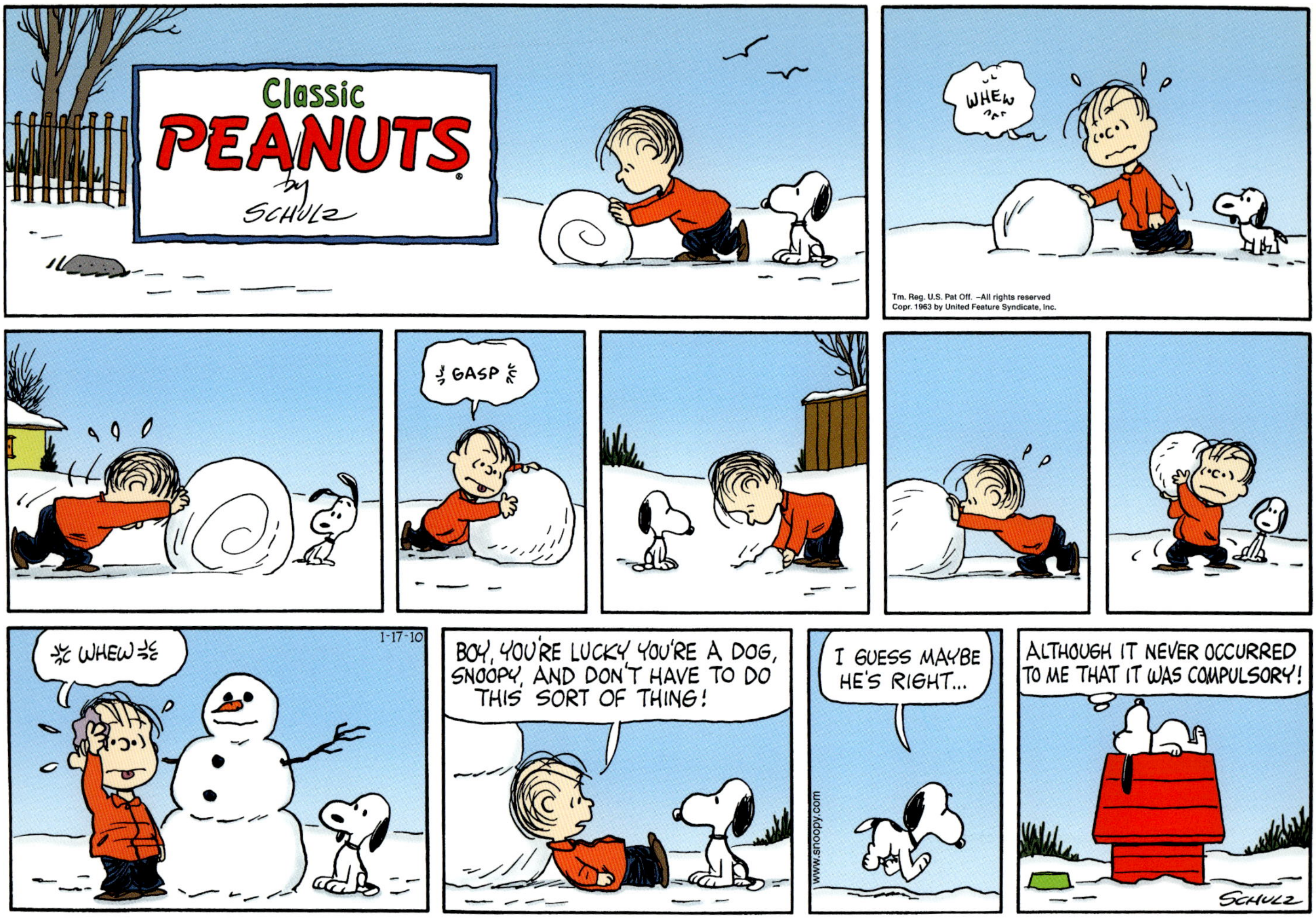

Classic
PEANUTS
by
SCHULZ
WHEW
Tm. Reg. U.S. Pat Off. –All rights reserved
Copr. 1963 by United Feature Syndicate, Inc.
GASP
WHEW
1-17-10
BOY, YOU'RE LUCKY YOU'RE A DOG, SNOOPY, AND DON'T HAVE TO DO THIS SORT OF THING!
www.snoopy.com
I GUESS MAYBE HE'S RIGHT...
ALTHOUGH IT NEVER OCCURRED TO ME THAT IT WAS COMPULSORY!
SCHULZ

NOTES

January 2013

S	M	T	W	T	F	S
		1	2	3	4	5
6	7	8	9	10	11	12
13	14	15	16	17	18	19
20	21	22	23	24	25	26
27	28	29	30	31		

JANUARY

14 MONDAY

15 TUESDAY

16 WEDNESDAY

17 THURSDAY

18 FRIDAY

19 SATURDAY

20 SUNDAY

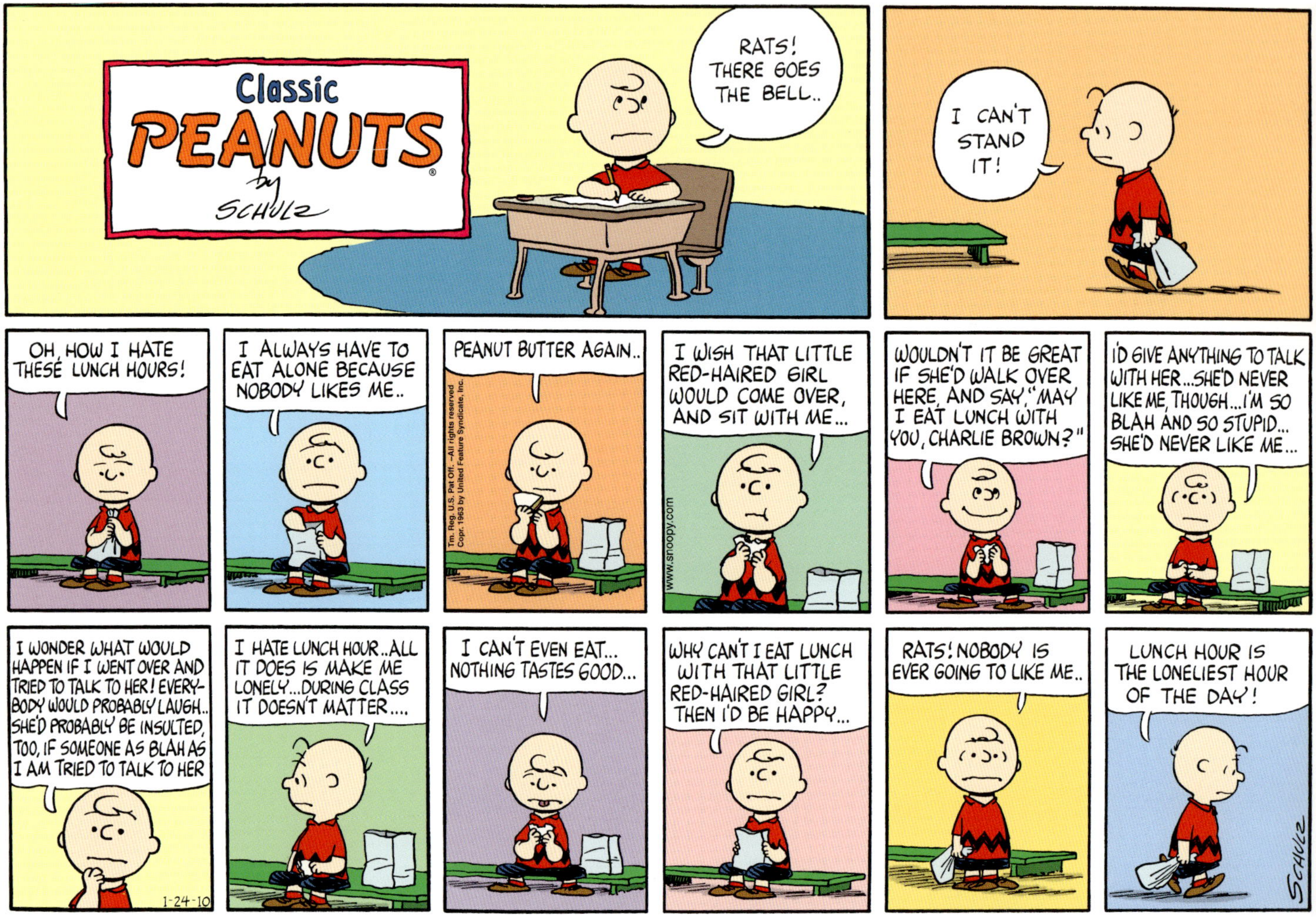
Classic
PEANUTS
by SCHULZ
RATS! THERE GOES THE BELL..
I CAN'T STAND IT!
OH, HOW I HATE THESE LUNCH HOURS!
I ALWAYS HAVE TO EAT ALONE BECAUSE NOBODY LIKES ME..
PEANUT BUTTER AGAIN..
Tm. Reg. U.S. Pat. Off. —All rights reserved
Copr. 1963 by United Feature Syndicate, Inc.
I WISH THAT LITTLE RED-HAIRED GIRL WOULD COME OVER, AND SIT WITH ME...
www.snoopy.com
WOULDN'T IT BE GREAT IF SHE'D WALK OVER HERE, AND SAY, "MAY I EAT LUNCH WITH YOU, CHARLIE BROWN?"
I'D GIVE ANYTHING TO TALK WITH HER...SHE'D NEVER LIKE ME, THOUGH...I'M SO BLAH AND SO STUPID... SHE'D NEVER LIKE ME...
I WONDER WHAT WOULD HAPPEN IF I WENT OVER AND TRIED TO TALK TO HER! EVERYBODY WOULD PROBABLY LAUGH.. SHE'D PROBABLY BE INSULTED, TOO, IF SOMEONE AS BLAH AS I AM TRIED TO TALK TO HER
1-24-10
I HATE LUNCH HOUR..ALL IT DOES IS MAKE ME LONELY...DURING CLASS IT DOESN'T MATTER....
I CAN'T EVEN EAT... NOTHING TASTES GOOD...
WHY CAN'T I EAT LUNCH WITH THAT LITTLE RED-HAIRED GIRL? THEN I'D BE HAPPY...
RATS! NOBODY IS EVER GOING TO LIKE ME..
LUNCH HOUR IS THE LONELIEST HOUR OF THE DAY!
SCHULZ

NOTES

January 2013

S	M	T	W	T	F	S
		1	2	3	4	5
6	7	8	9	10	11	12
13	14	15	16	17	18	19
20	21	22	23	24	25	26
27	28	29	30	31		

JANUARY

21 MONDAY

Martin Luther King Jr.'s Birthday (observed) (USA)

22 TUESDAY

23 WEDNESDAY

24 THURSDAY

25 FRIDAY

26 SATURDAY

Australia Day

27 SUNDAY

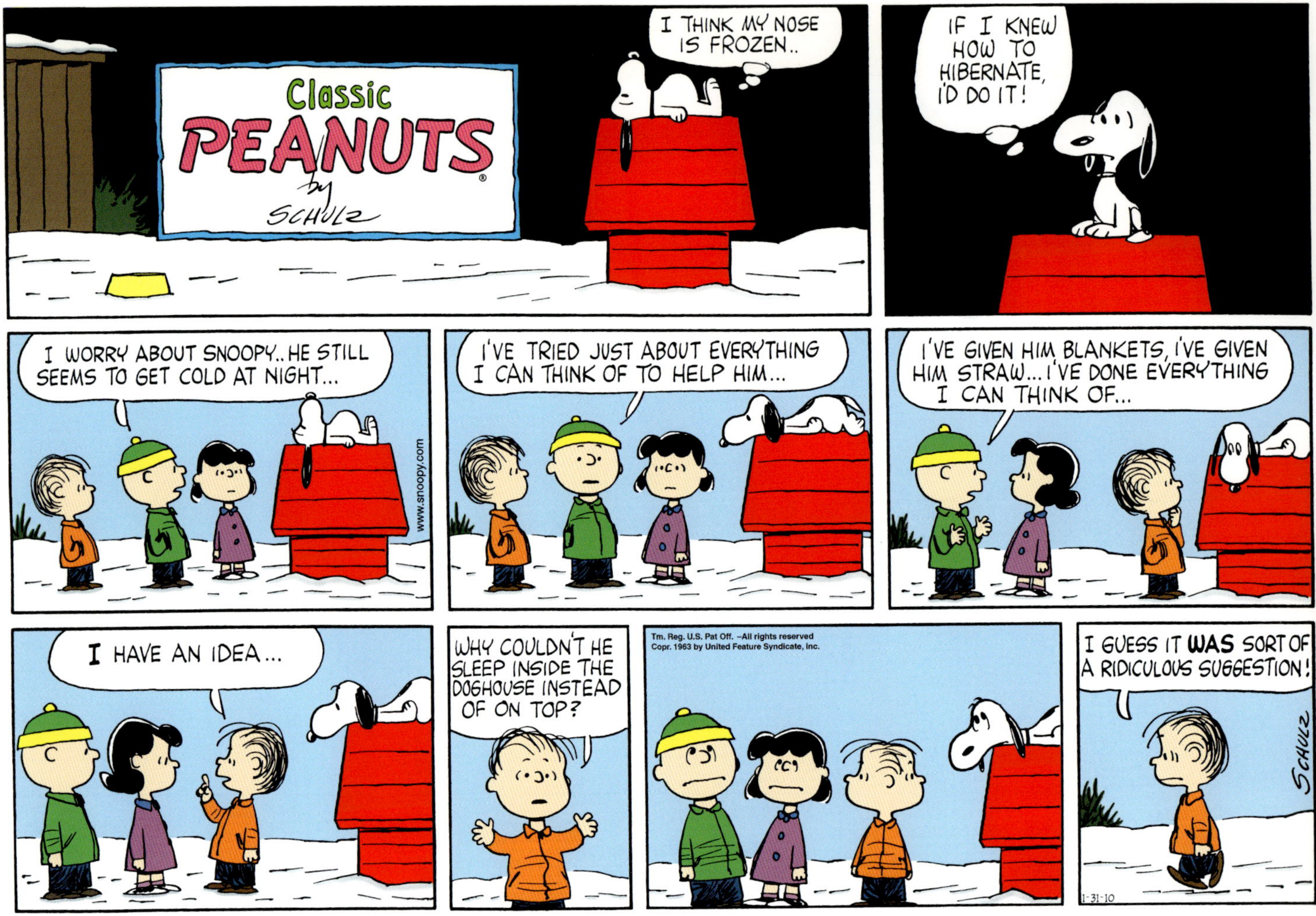
Classic
PEANUTS
by SCHULZ
I THINK MY NOSE IS FROZEN..
IF I KNEW HOW TO HIBERNATE, I'D DO IT!
I WORRY ABOUT SNOOPY..HE STILL SEEMS TO GET COLD AT NIGHT...
www.snoopy.com
I'VE TRIED JUST ABOUT EVERYTHING I CAN THINK OF TO HELP HIM...
I'VE GIVEN HIM BLANKETS, I'VE GIVEN HIM STRAW... I'VE DONE EVERYTHING I CAN THINK OF...
I HAVE AN IDEA...
WHY COULDN'T HE SLEEP INSIDE THE DOGHOUSE INSTEAD OF ON TOP?
Tm. Reg. U.S. Pat Off. –All rights reserved
Copr. 1963 by United Feature Syndicate, Inc.
I GUESS IT **WAS** SORT OF A RIDICULOUS SUGGESTION!
SCHULZ
1-31-10

NOTES

January 2013

S	M	T	W	T	F	S
		1	2	3	4	5
6	7	8	9	10	11	12
13	14	15	16	17	18	19
20	21	22	23	24	25	26
27	28	29	30	31		

February 2013

S	M	T	W	T	F	S
					1	2
3	4	5	6	7	8	9
10	11	12	13	14	15	16
17	18	19	20	21	22	23
24	25	26	27	28		

JANUARY–FEBRUARY

28 MONDAY

Australia Day (observed)
(Australia—except NSW)

29 TUESDAY

30 WEDNESDAY

31 THURSDAY

1 FRIDAY

2 SATURDAY

3 SUNDAY

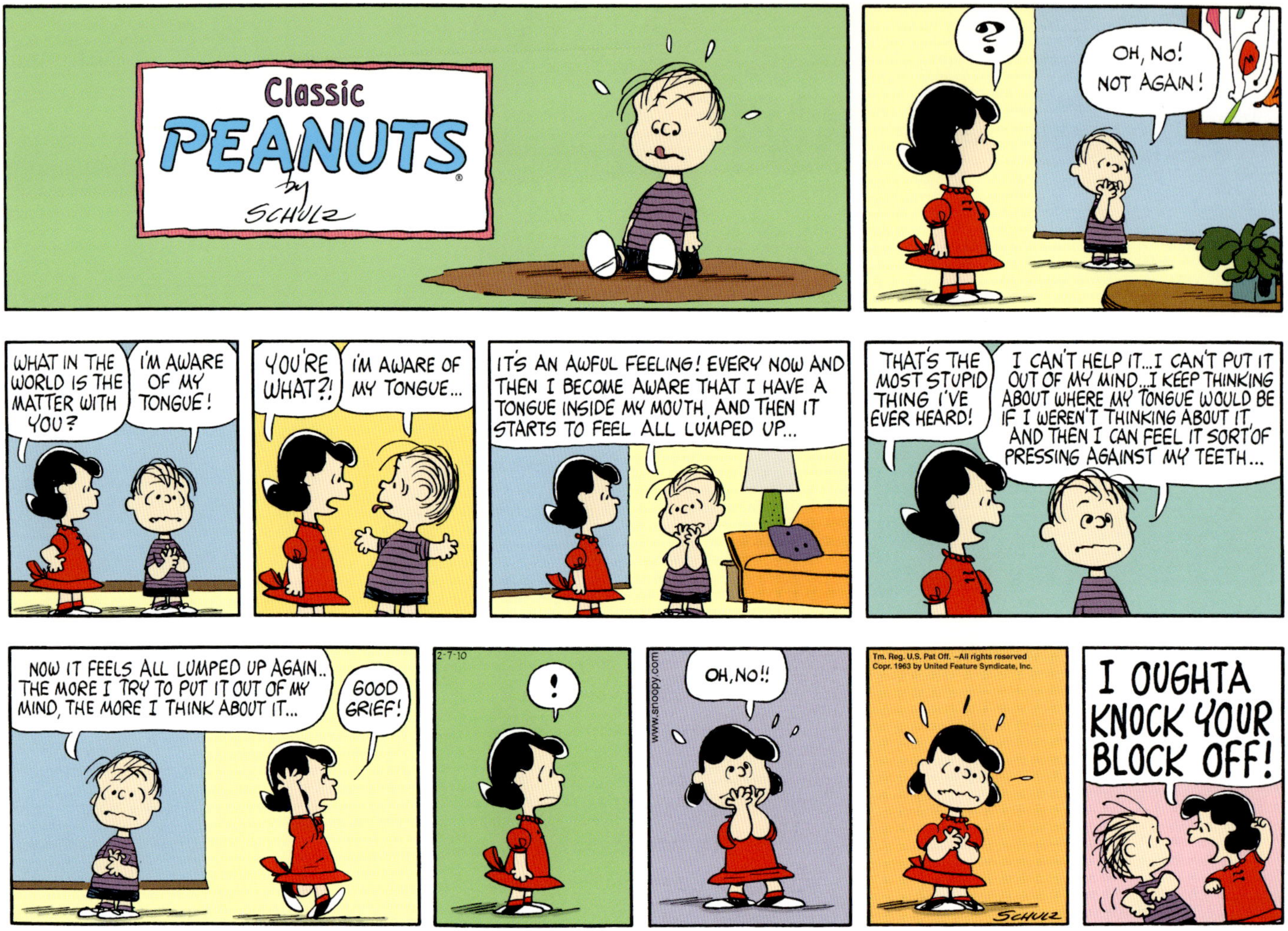
Classic
PEANUTS
by SCHULZ
?
OH, NO! NOT AGAIN!
WHAT IN THE WORLD IS THE MATTER WITH YOU?
I'M AWARE OF MY TONGUE!
YOU'RE WHAT?!
I'M AWARE OF MY TONGUE...
IT'S AN AWFUL FEELING! EVERY NOW AND THEN I BECOME AWARE THAT I HAVE A TONGUE INSIDE MY MOUTH, AND THEN IT STARTS TO FEEL ALL LUMPED UP...
THAT'S THE MOST STUPID THING I'VE EVER HEARD!
I CAN'T HELP IT...I CAN'T PUT IT OUT OF MY MIND...I KEEP THINKING ABOUT WHERE MY TONGUE WOULD BE IF I WEREN'T THINKING ABOUT IT, AND THEN I CAN FEEL IT SORT OF PRESSING AGAINST MY TEETH...
NOW IT FEELS ALL LUMPED UP AGAIN.. THE MORE I TRY TO PUT IT OUT OF MY MIND, THE MORE I THINK ABOUT IT...
GOOD GRIEF!
2-7-10
!
www.snoopy.com
OH, NO!!
Tm. Reg. U.S. Pat Off. –All rights reserved
Copr. 1963 by United Feature Syndicate, Inc.
SCHULZ
I OUGHTA KNOCK YOUR BLOCK OFF!

NOTES

February 2013

S	M	T	W	T	F	S
					1	2
3	4	5	6	7	8	9
10	11	12	13	14	15	16
17	18	19	20	21	22	23
24	25	26	27	28		

FEBRUARY

4 MONDAY

5 TUESDAY

6 WEDNESDAY

Waitangi Day (NZ)

7 THURSDAY

8 FRIDAY

9 SATURDAY

10 SUNDAY

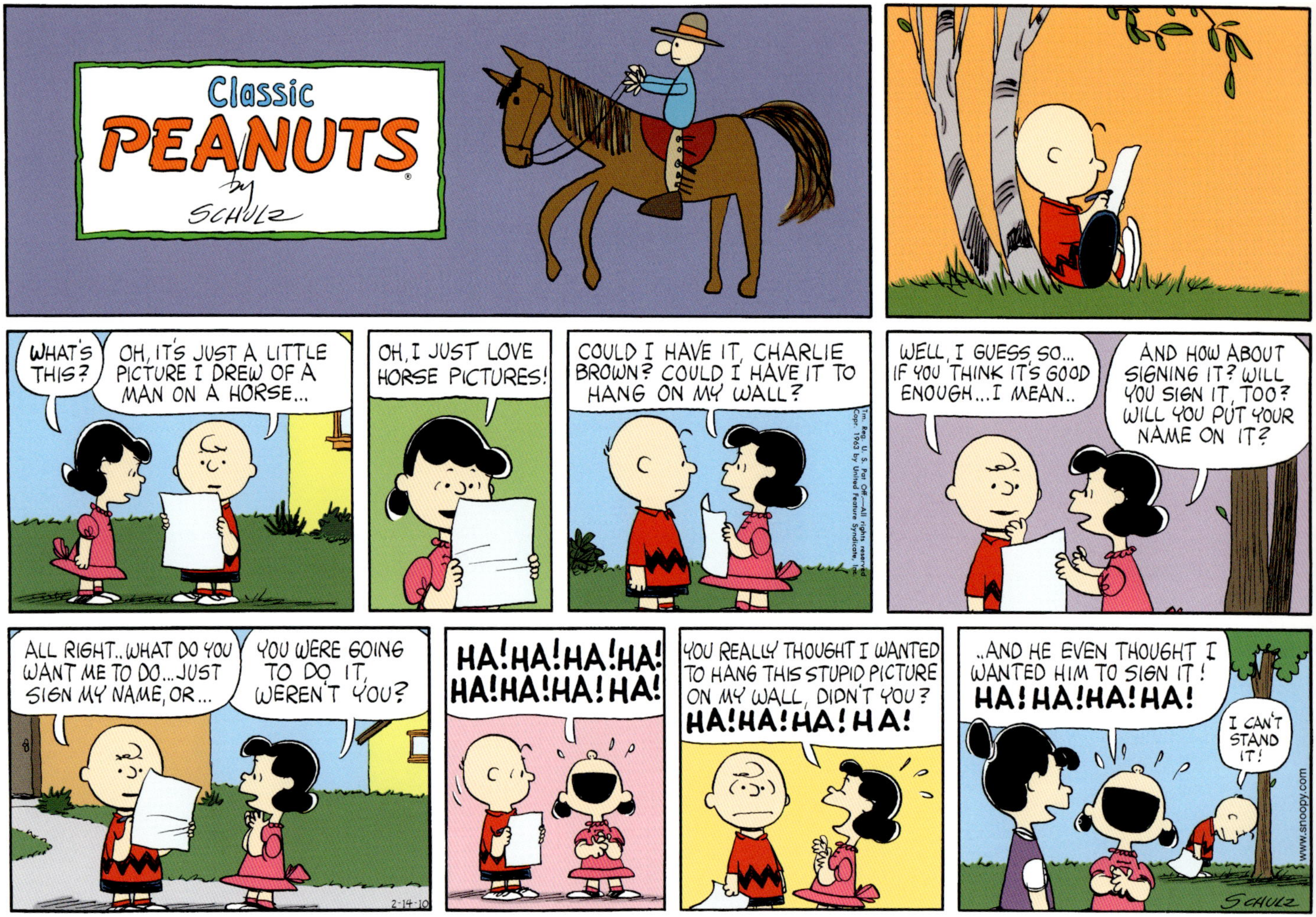
Classic
PEANUTS
by SCHULZ
WHAT'S THIS?
OH, IT'S JUST A LITTLE PICTURE I DREW OF A MAN ON A HORSE...
OH, I JUST LOVE HORSE PICTURES!
COULD I HAVE IT, CHARLIE BROWN? COULD I HAVE IT TO HANG ON MY WALL?
Tm. Reg. U. S. Pat. Off.—All rights reserved
Copr. 1963 by United Feature Syndicate, Inc.
WELL, I GUESS SO... IF YOU THINK IT'S GOOD ENOUGH... I MEAN..
AND HOW ABOUT SIGNING IT? WILL YOU SIGN IT, TOO? WILL YOU PUT YOUR NAME ON IT?
ALL RIGHT.. WHAT DO YOU WANT ME TO DO... JUST SIGN MY NAME, OR...
YOU WERE GOING TO DO IT, WEREN'T YOU?
2-14-10
HA! HA! HA! HA! HA! HA! HA! HA!
YOU REALLY THOUGHT I WANTED TO HANG THIS STUPID PICTURE ON MY WALL, DIDN'T YOU? HA! HA! HA! HA!
..AND HE EVEN THOUGHT I WANTED HIM TO SIGN IT! HA! HA! HA! HA!
I CAN'T STAND IT!
www.snoopy.com
SCHULZ

NOTES

February 2013

S	M	T	W	T	F	S
					1	2
3	4	5	6	7	8	9
10	11	12	13	14	15	16
17	18	19	20	21	22	23
24	25	26	27	28		

FEBRUARY

11 MONDAY

12 TUESDAY

13 WEDNESDAY

Ash Wednesday

14 THURSDAY

St. Valentine's Day

15 FRIDAY

16 SATURDAY

17 SUNDAY

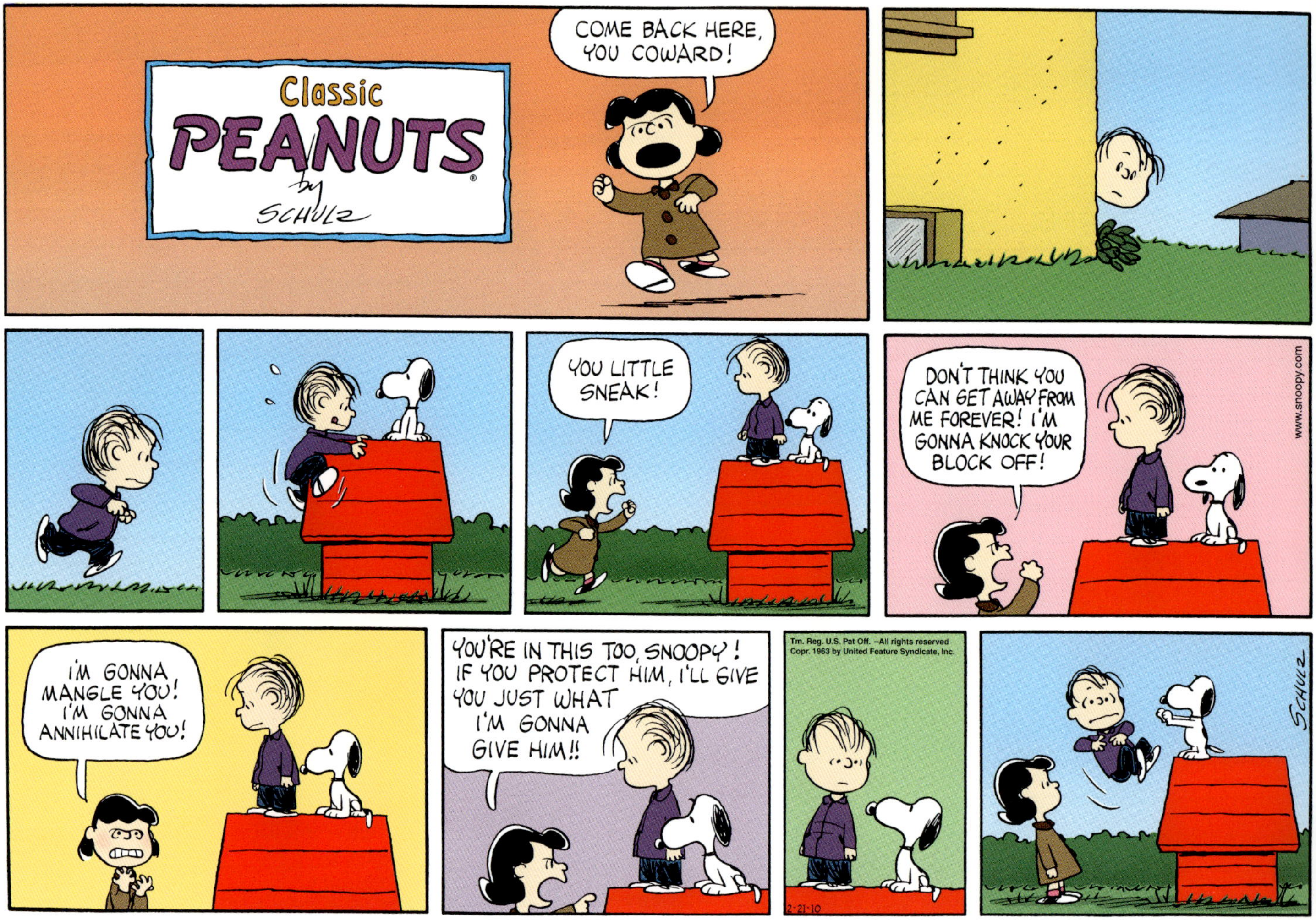
Classic PEANUTS by SCHULZ
COME BACK HERE, YOU COWARD!
YOU LITTLE SNEAK!
DON'T THINK YOU CAN GET AWAY FROM ME FOREVER! I'M GONNA KNOCK YOUR BLOCK OFF!
www.snoopy.com
I'M GONNA MANGLE YOU! I'M GONNA ANNIHILATE YOU!
YOU'RE IN THIS TOO, SNOOPY! IF YOU PROTECT HIM, I'LL GIVE YOU JUST WHAT I'M GONNA GIVE HIM!!
Tm. Reg. U.S. Pat Off. –All rights reserved
Copr. 1963 by United Feature Syndicate, Inc.
2-21-10
SCHULZ

NOTES

February 2013

S	M	T	W	T	F	S
					1	2
3	4	5	6	7	8	9
10	11	12	13	14	15	16
17	18	19	20	21	22	23
24	25	26	27	28		

FEBRUARY

18 MONDAY

Presidents' Day (USA)

19 TUESDAY

20 WEDNESDAY

21 THURSDAY

22 FRIDAY

23 SATURDAY

24 SUNDAY

*Purim**

*Begins at sundown the previous day

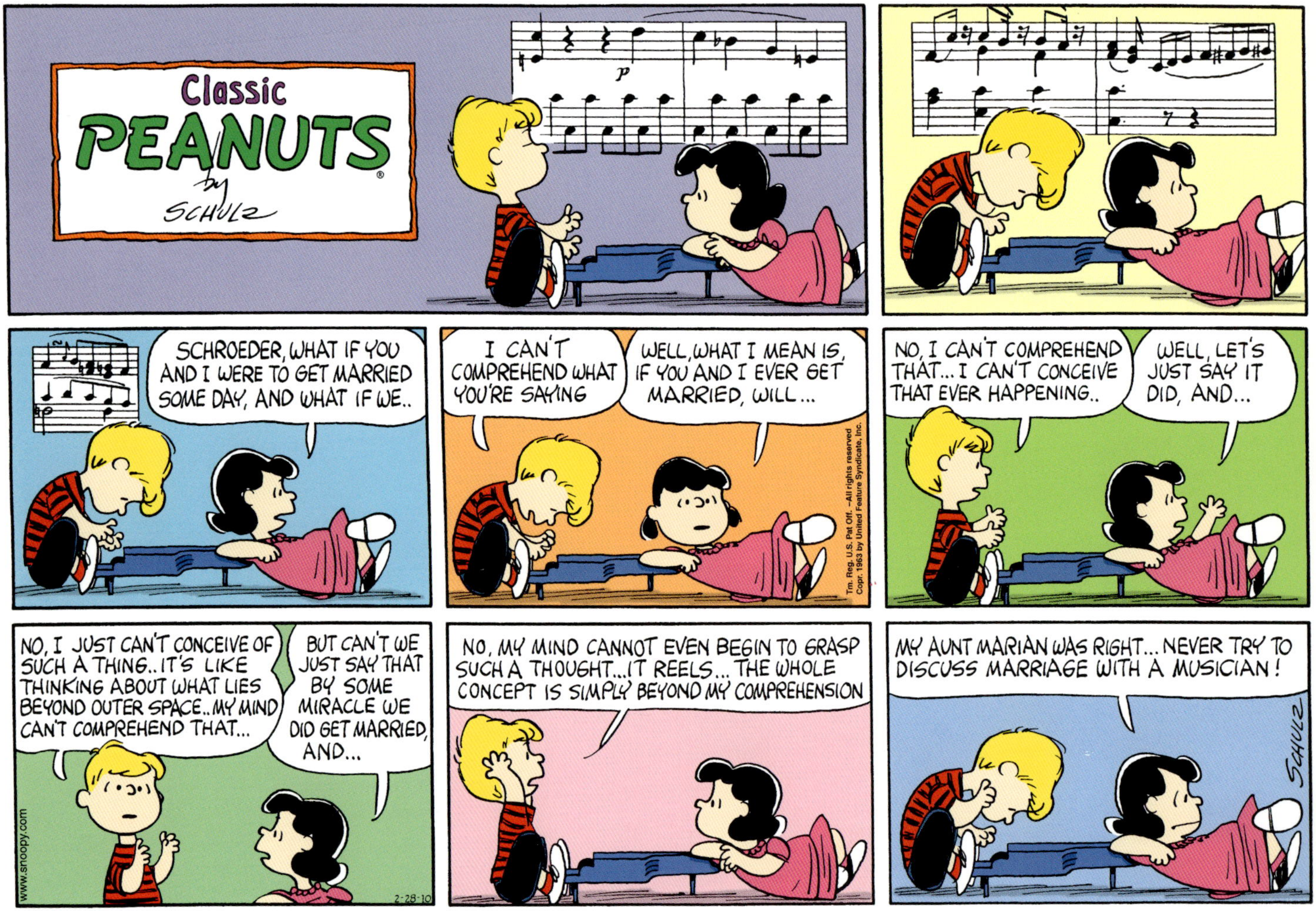
Classic PEANUTS by SCHULZ
SCHROEDER, WHAT IF YOU AND I WERE TO GET MARRIED SOME DAY, AND WHAT IF WE..
I CAN'T COMPREHEND WHAT YOU'RE SAYING
WELL, WHAT I MEAN IS, IF YOU AND I EVER GET MARRIED, WILL...
Tm. Reg. U.S. Pat. Off.—All rights reserved
Copr. 1963 by United Feature Syndicate, Inc.
NO, I CAN'T COMPREHEND THAT... I CAN'T CONCEIVE THAT EVER HAPPENING..
WELL, LET'S JUST SAY IT DID, AND...
NO, I JUST CAN'T CONCEIVE OF SUCH A THING.. IT'S LIKE THINKING ABOUT WHAT LIES BEYOND OUTER SPACE.. MY MIND CAN'T COMPREHEND THAT...
BUT CAN'T WE JUST SAY THAT BY SOME MIRACLE WE DID GET MARRIED, AND...
www.snoopy.com
2-28-10
NO, MY MIND CANNOT EVEN BEGIN TO GRASP SUCH A THOUGHT... IT REELS... THE WHOLE CONCEPT IS SIMPLY BEYOND MY COMPREHENSION
MY AUNT MARIAN WAS RIGHT... NEVER TRY TO DISCUSS MARRIAGE WITH A MUSICIAN!
SCHULZ

NOTES

February 2013

S	M	T	W	T	F	S
					1	2
3	4	5	6	7	8	9
10	11	12	13	14	15	16
17	18	19	20	21	22	23
24	25	26	27	28		

March 2013

S	M	T	W	T	F	S
					1	2
3	4	5	6	7	8	9
10	11	12	13	14	15	16
17	18	19	20	21	22	23
24	25	26	27	28	29	30
31						

FEBRUARY–MARCH

25 MONDAY

26 TUESDAY

27 WEDNESDAY

28 THURSDAY

1 FRIDAY

St. David's Day (UK)

2 SATURDAY

3 SUNDAY

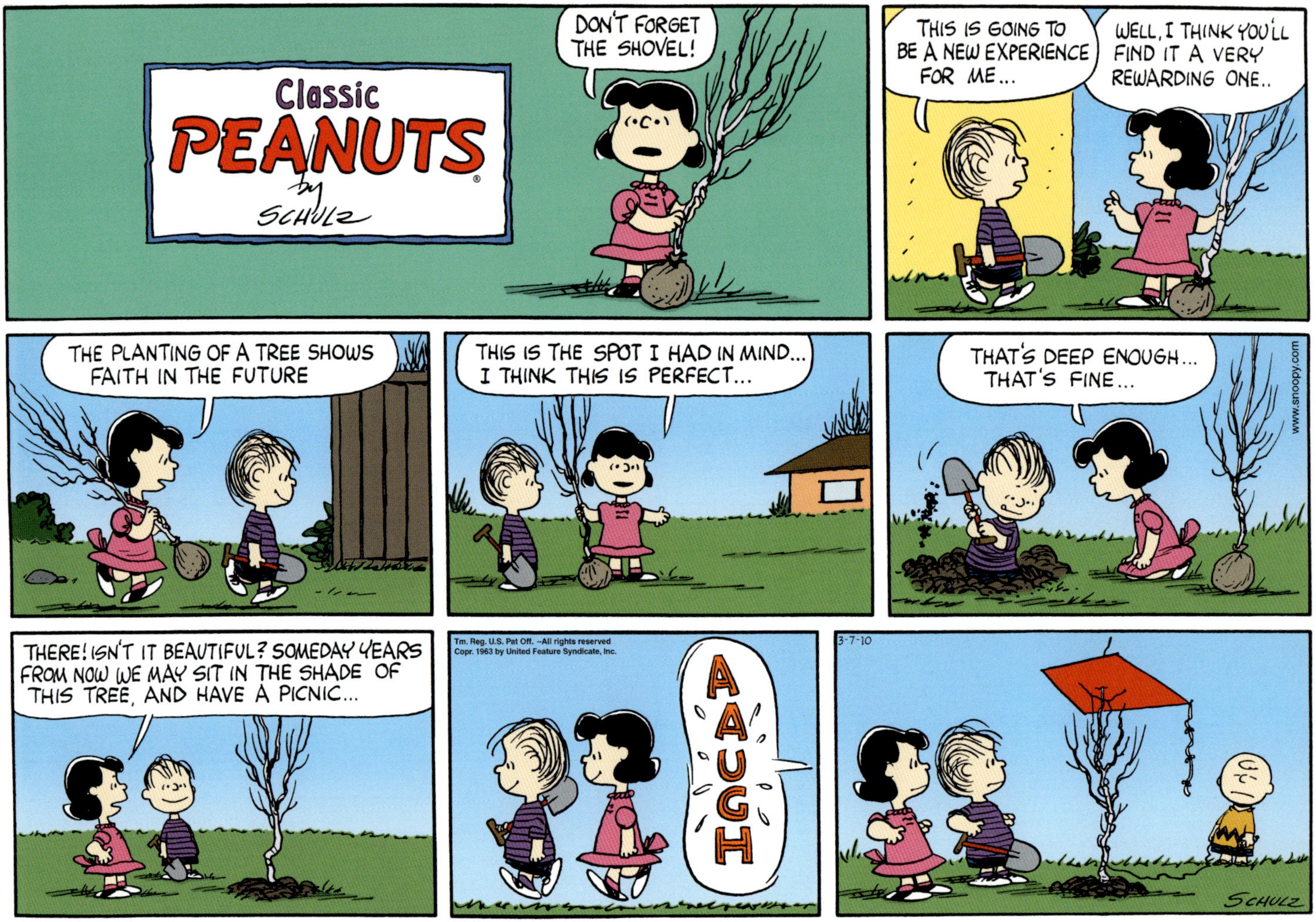
Classic
PEANUTS
by
SCHULZ
DON'T FORGET THE SHOVEL!
THIS IS GOING TO BE A NEW EXPERIENCE FOR ME...
WELL, I THINK YOU'LL FIND IT A VERY REWARDING ONE..
THE PLANTING OF A TREE SHOWS FAITH IN THE FUTURE
THIS IS THE SPOT I HAD IN MIND... I THINK THIS IS PERFECT...
THAT'S DEEP ENOUGH... THAT'S FINE...
www.snoopy.com
THERE! ISN'T IT BEAUTIFUL? SOMEDAY YEARS FROM NOW WE MAY SIT IN THE SHADE OF THIS TREE, AND HAVE A PICNIC...
Tm. Reg. U.S. Pat Off. –All rights reserved
Copr. 1963 by United Feature Syndicate, Inc.
AAUGH
3-7-10
SCHULZ

NOTES

March 2013

S	M	T	W	T	F	S
					1	2
3	4	5	6	7	8	9
10	11	12	13	14	15	16
17	18	19	20	21	22	23
24	25	26	27	28	29	30
31						

MARCH

4 MONDAY

Labour Day (Australia—WA)

5 TUESDAY

6 WEDNESDAY

7 THURSDAY

8 FRIDAY

International Women's Day

9 SATURDAY

10 SUNDAY

Mothering Sunday (Ireland, UK)

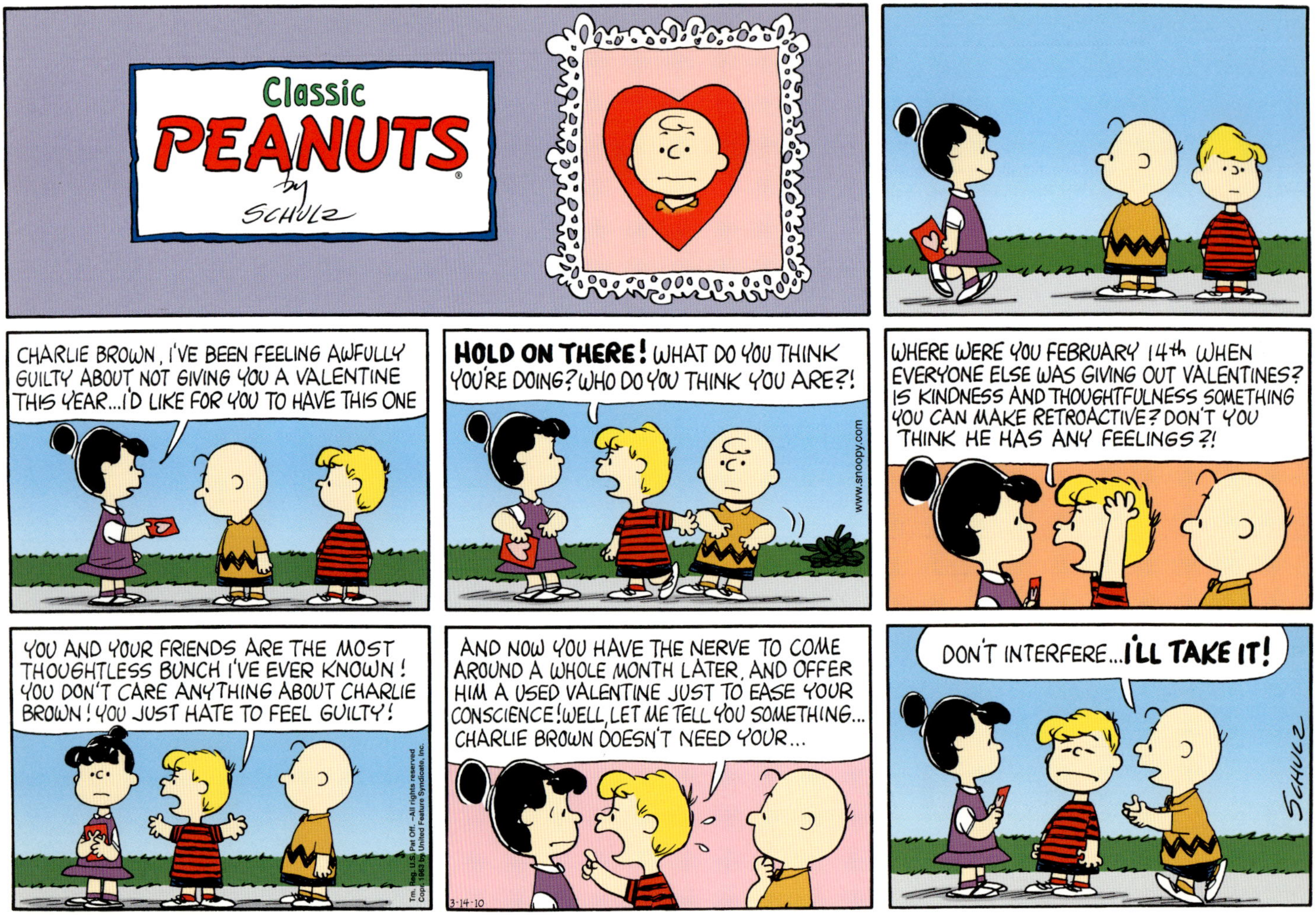
Classic PEANUTS by SCHULZ
CHARLIE BROWN, I'VE BEEN FEELING AWFULLY GUILTY ABOUT NOT GIVING YOU A VALENTINE THIS YEAR...I'D LIKE FOR YOU TO HAVE THIS ONE
HOLD ON THERE! WHAT DO YOU THINK YOU'RE DOING? WHO DO YOU THINK YOU ARE?!
www.snoopy.com
WHERE WERE YOU FEBRUARY 14th WHEN EVERYONE ELSE WAS GIVING OUT VALENTINES? IS KINDNESS AND THOUGHTFULNESS SOMETHING YOU CAN MAKE RETROACTIVE? DON'T YOU THINK HE HAS ANY FEELINGS?!
YOU AND YOUR FRIENDS ARE THE MOST THOUGHTLESS BUNCH I'VE EVER KNOWN! YOU DON'T CARE ANYTHING ABOUT CHARLIE BROWN! YOU JUST HATE TO FEEL GUILTY!
Tm. Reg. U.S. Pat. Off.—All rights reserved Copr. 1963 by United Feature Syndicate, Inc.
AND NOW YOU HAVE THE NERVE TO COME AROUND A WHOLE MONTH LATER, AND OFFER HIM A USED VALENTINE JUST TO EASE YOUR CONSCIENCE! WELL, LET ME TELL YOU SOMETHING... CHARLIE BROWN DOESN'T NEED YOUR...
3-14-10
DON'T INTERFERE...I'LL TAKE IT!
SCHULZ

NOTES

March 2013

S	M	T	W	T	F	S
					1	2
3	4	5	6	7	8	9
10	11	12	13	14	15	16
17	18	19	20	21	22	23
24	25	26	27	28	29	30
31						

MARCH

11 MONDAY

Eight Hours Day (Australia—TAS)

Canberra Day (Australia—ACT)

Labour Day (Australia—VIC)

Commonwealth Day (Australia, Canada, NZ, UK)

12 TUESDAY

13 WEDNESDAY

14 THURSDAY

15 FRIDAY

16 SATURDAY

17 SUNDAY

St. Patrick's Day

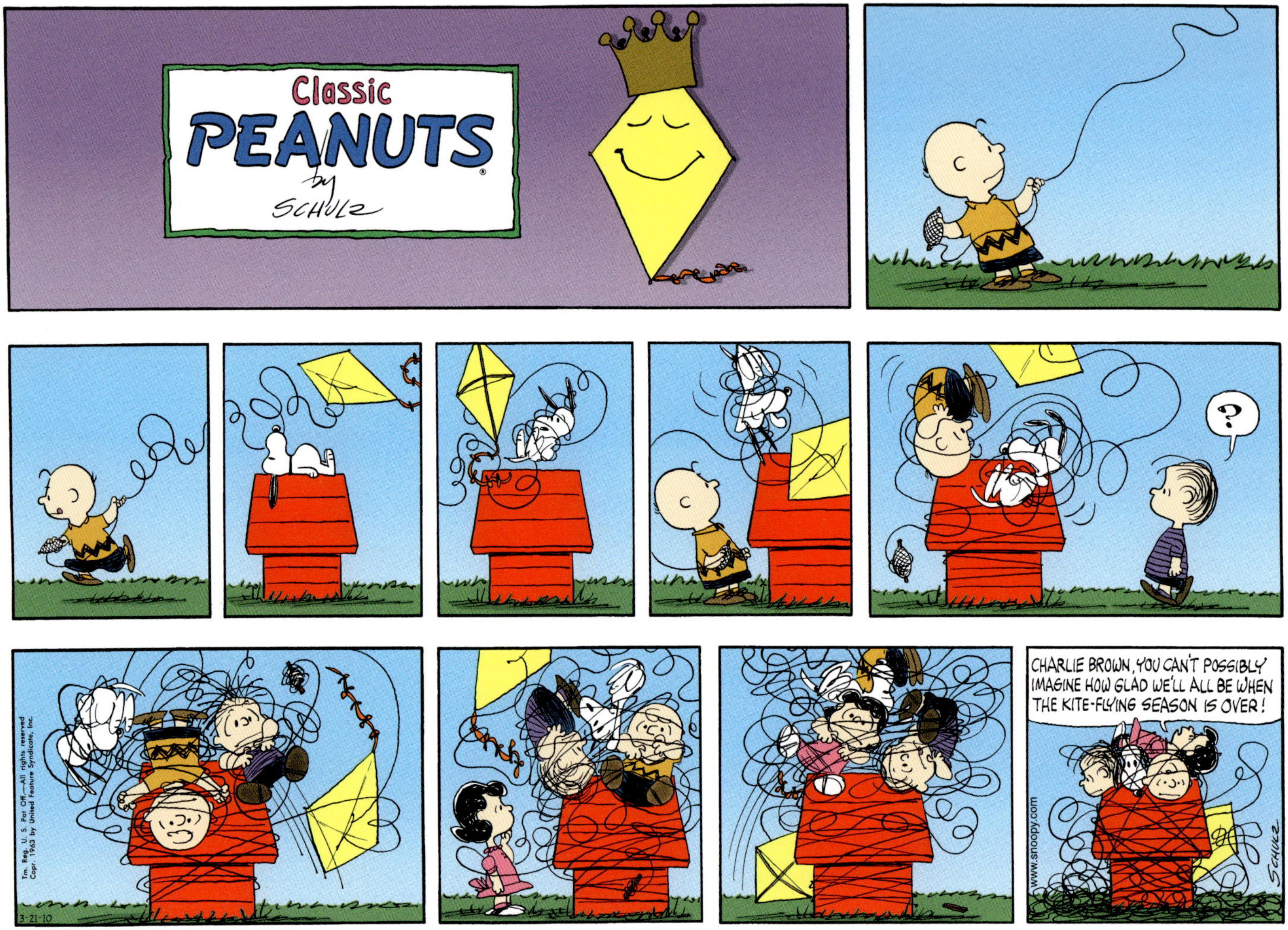
Classic
PEANUTS
by
SCHULZ
?
CHARLIE BROWN, YOU CAN'T POSSIBLY IMAGINE HOW GLAD WE'LL ALL BE WHEN THE KITE-FLYING SEASON IS OVER!
Tm. Reg. U. S. Pat Off.—All rights reserved
Copr. 1963 by United Feature Syndicate, Inc.
3-21-10
www.snoopy.com
SCHULZ

NOTES

March 2013

S	M	T	W	T	F	S
					1	2
3	4	5	6	7	8	9
10	11	12	13	14	15	16
17	18	19	20	21	22	23
24	25	26	27	28	29	30
31						

MARCH

18 MONDAY

19 TUESDAY

20 WEDNESDAY

21 THURSDAY

22 FRIDAY

23 SATURDAY

24 SUNDAY

Palm Sunday

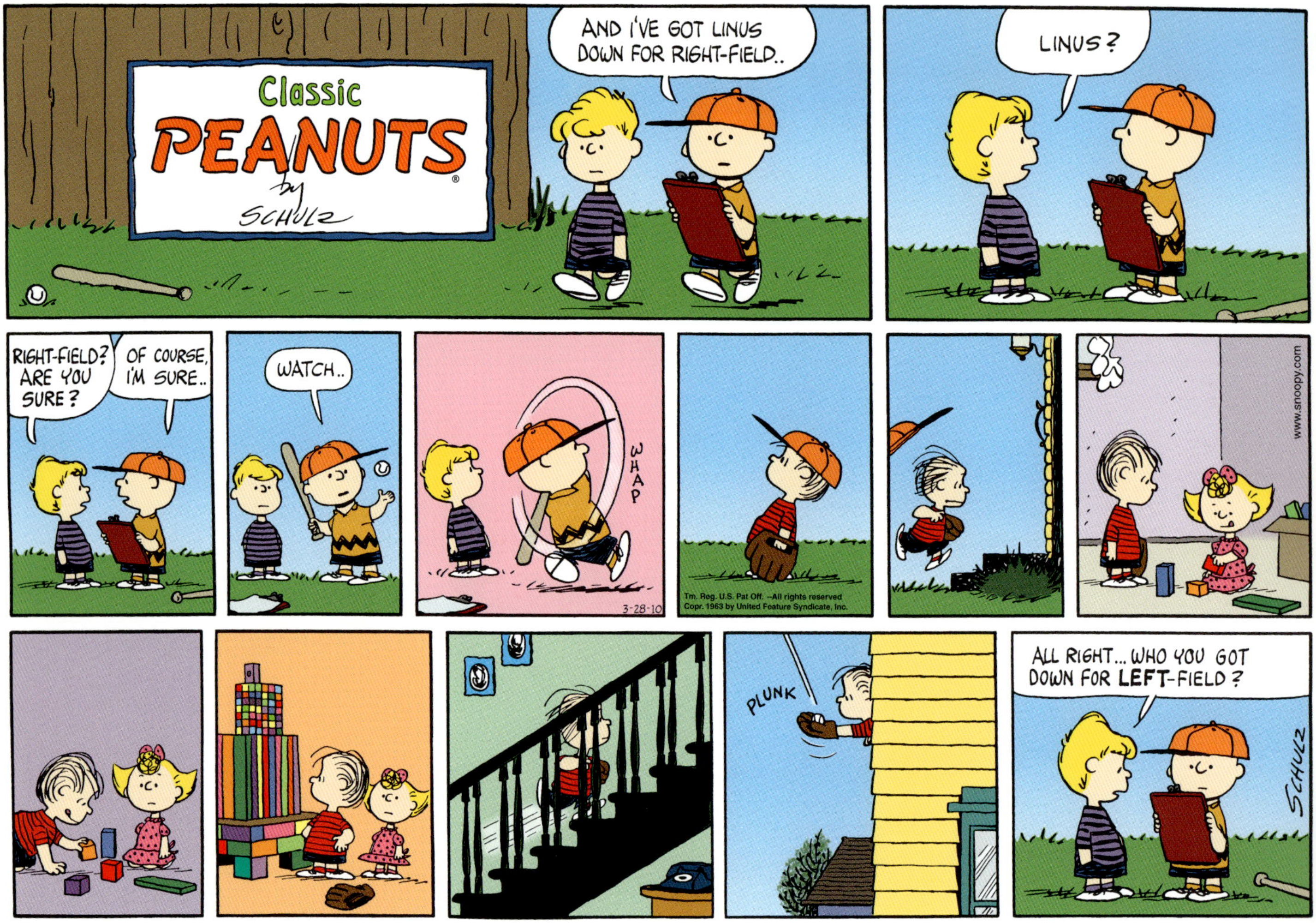
Classic PEANUTS by SCHULZ
AND I'VE GOT LINUS DOWN FOR RIGHT-FIELD..
LINUS?
RIGHT-FIELD? ARE YOU SURE?
OF COURSE, I'M SURE..
WATCH..
WHAP
3-28-10
Tm. Reg. U.S. Pat Off. --All rights reserved
Copr. 1963 by United Feature Syndicate, Inc.
www.snoopy.com
PLUNK
ALL RIGHT... WHO YOU GOT DOWN FOR **LEFT**-FIELD?
SCHULZ

NOTES

March 2013

S	M	T	W	T	F	S
					1	2
3	4	5	6	7	8	9
10	11	12	13	14	15	16
17	18	19	20	21	22	23
24	25	26	27	28	29	30
31						

MARCH

25 MONDAY

26 TUESDAY

*Passover**

27 WEDNESDAY

28 THURSDAY

29 FRIDAY

Good Friday (Western)

30 SATURDAY

Easter Saturday (Australia—except TAS, WA)

31 SUNDAY

Easter (Western)

**Begins at sundown the previous day*

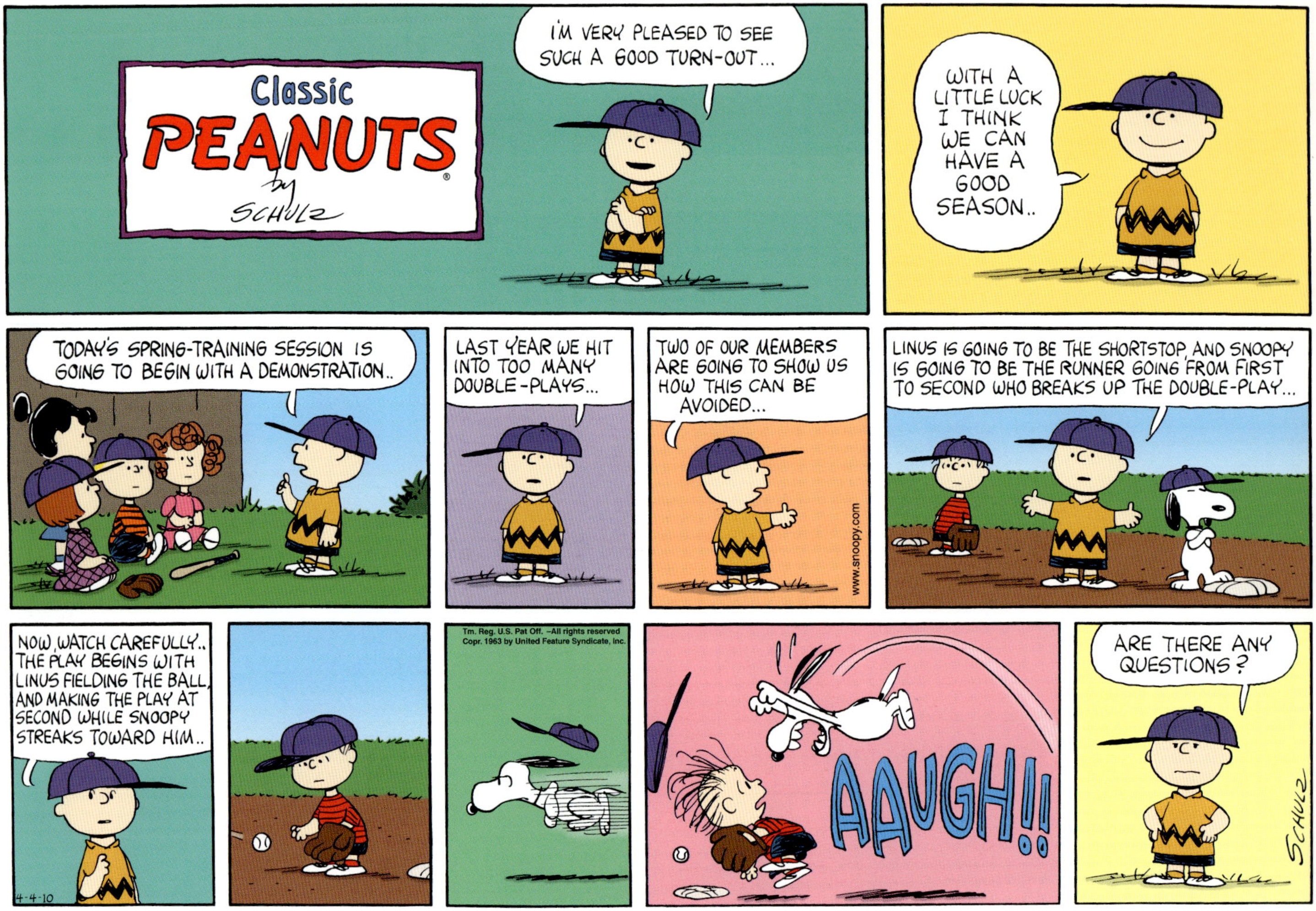
Classic
PEANUTS
by SCHULZ
I'M VERY PLEASED TO SEE SUCH A GOOD TURN-OUT...
WITH A LITTLE LUCK I THINK WE CAN HAVE A GOOD SEASON..
TODAY'S SPRING-TRAINING SESSION IS GOING TO BEGIN WITH A DEMONSTRATION..
LAST YEAR WE HIT INTO TOO MANY DOUBLE-PLAYS...
TWO OF OUR MEMBERS ARE GOING TO SHOW US HOW THIS CAN BE AVOIDED...
www.snoopy.com
LINUS IS GOING TO BE THE SHORTSTOP, AND SNOOPY IS GOING TO BE THE RUNNER GOING FROM FIRST TO SECOND WHO BREAKS UP THE DOUBLE-PLAY...
NOW, WATCH CAREFULLY.. THE PLAY BEGINS WITH LINUS FIELDING THE BALL, AND MAKING THE PLAY AT SECOND WHILE SNOOPY STREAKS TOWARD HIM..
4-4-10
Tm. Reg. U.S. Pat Off. –All rights reserved
Copr. 1963 by United Feature Syndicate, Inc.
AAUGH!!
ARE THERE ANY QUESTIONS?
SCHULZ

NOTES

April 2013

S	M	T	W	T	F	S
	1	2	3	4	5	6
7	8	9	10	11	12	13
14	15	16	17	18	19	20
21	22	23	24	25	26	27
28	29	30				

APRIL

1 MONDAY

Easter Monday (Australia, Canada, Ireland, NZ, UK—except Scotland)

2 TUESDAY

Passover ends

3 WEDNESDAY

4 THURSDAY

5 FRIDAY

6 SATURDAY

7 SUNDAY

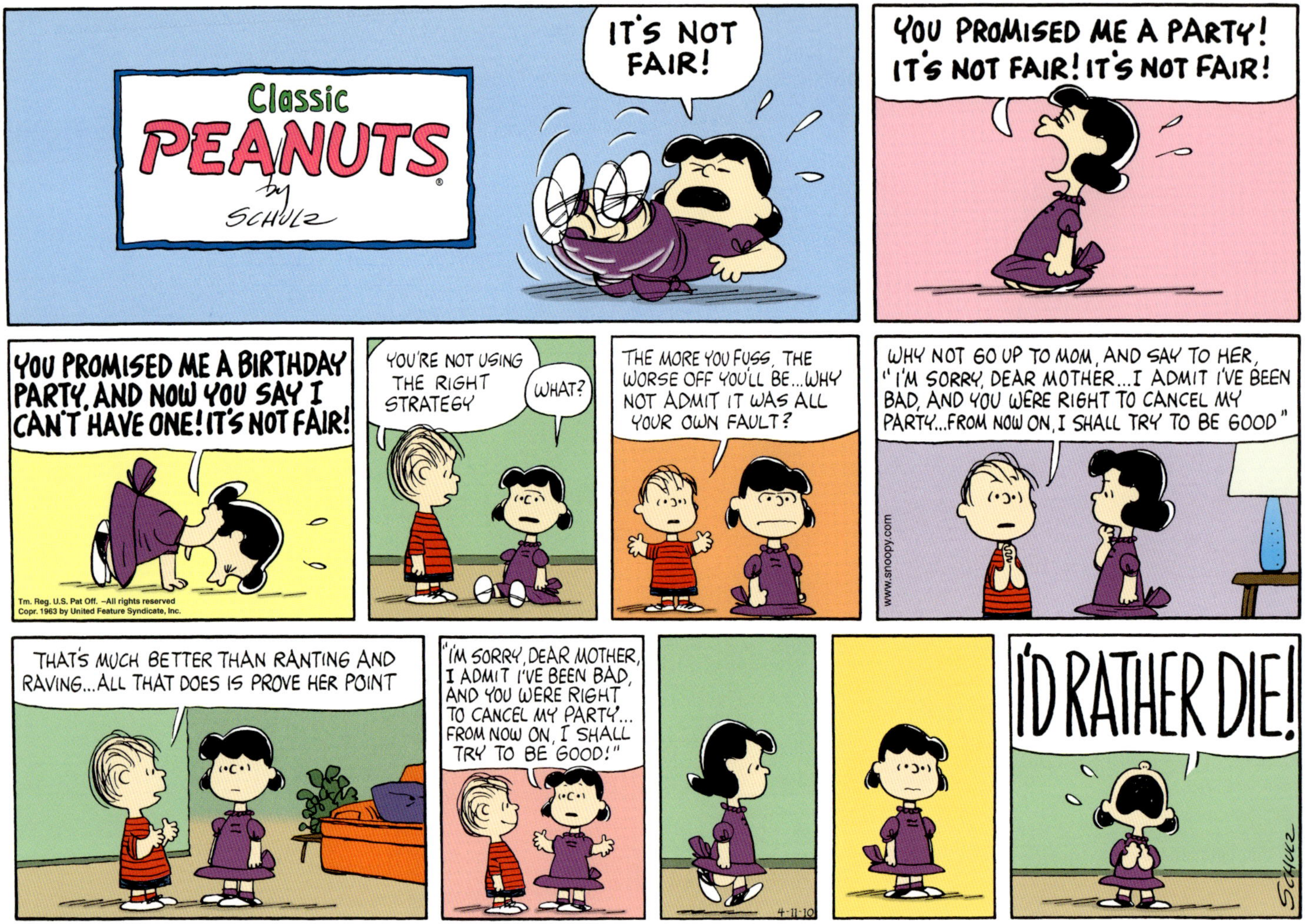
Classic
PEANUTS
by SCHULZ
IT'S NOT FAIR!
YOU PROMISED ME A PARTY! IT'S NOT FAIR! IT'S NOT FAIR!
YOU PROMISED ME A BIRTHDAY PARTY, AND NOW YOU SAY I CAN'T HAVE ONE! IT'S NOT FAIR!
Tm. Reg. U.S. Pat Off. –All rights reserved
Copr. 1963 by United Feature Syndicate, Inc.
YOU'RE NOT USING THE RIGHT STRATEGY
WHAT?
THE MORE YOU FUSS, THE WORSE OFF YOU'LL BE...WHY NOT ADMIT IT WAS ALL YOUR OWN FAULT?
www.snoopy.com
WHY NOT GO UP TO MOM, AND SAY TO HER, "I'M SORRY, DEAR MOTHER...I ADMIT I'VE BEEN BAD, AND YOU WERE RIGHT TO CANCEL MY PARTY...FROM NOW ON, I SHALL TRY TO BE GOOD"
THAT'S MUCH BETTER THAN RANTING AND RAVING...ALL THAT DOES IS PROVE HER POINT
"I'M SORRY, DEAR MOTHER, I ADMIT I'VE BEEN BAD, AND YOU WERE RIGHT TO CANCEL MY PARTY... FROM NOW ON, I SHALL TRY TO BE GOOD!"
4-11-10
I'D RATHER DIE!
SCHULZ

NOTES

April 2013

S	M	T	W	T	F	S
	1	2	3	4	5	6
7	8	9	10	11	12	13
14	15	16	17	18	19	20
21	22	23	24	25	26	27
28	29	30				

APRIL

8 MONDAY

9 TUESDAY

10 WEDNESDAY

11 THURSDAY

12 FRIDAY

13 SATURDAY

14 SUNDAY

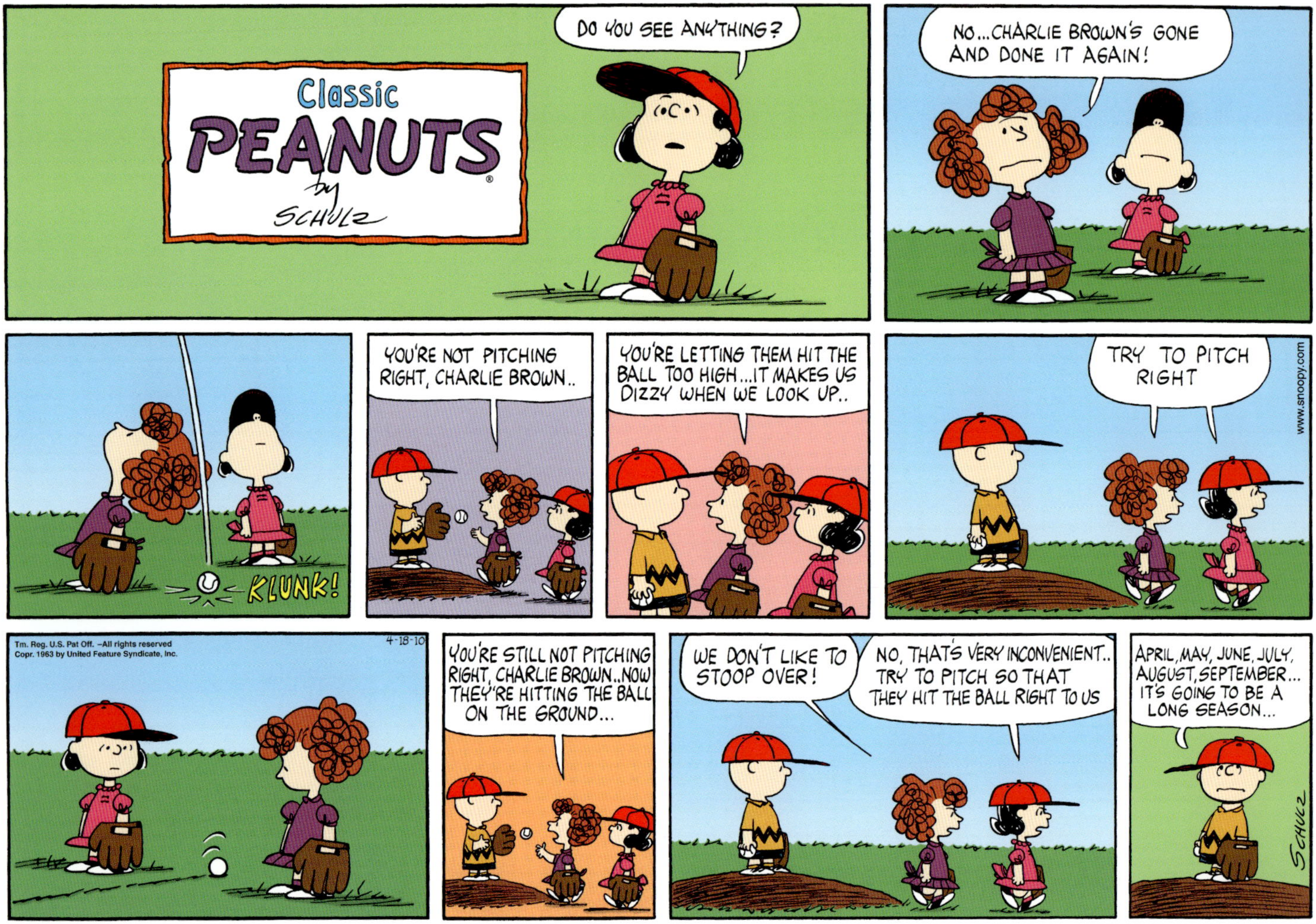
Classic
PEANUTS
by SCHULZ
DO YOU SEE ANYTHING?
NO...CHARLIE BROWN'S GONE AND DONE IT AGAIN!
KLUNK!
YOU'RE NOT PITCHING RIGHT, CHARLIE BROWN..
YOU'RE LETTING THEM HIT THE BALL TOO HIGH...IT MAKES US DIZZY WHEN WE LOOK UP..
TRY TO PITCH RIGHT
www.snoopy.com
Tm. Reg. U.S. Pat Off. –All rights reserved
Copr. 1963 by United Feature Syndicate, Inc.
4-18-10
YOU'RE STILL NOT PITCHING RIGHT, CHARLIE BROWN..NOW THEY'RE HITTING THE BALL ON THE GROUND...
WE DON'T LIKE TO STOOP OVER!
NO, THAT'S VERY INCONVENIENT.. TRY TO PITCH SO THAT THEY HIT THE BALL RIGHT TO US
APRIL, MAY, JUNE, JULY, AUGUST, SEPTEMBER... IT'S GOING TO BE A LONG SEASON...
SCHULZ

NOTES

April 2013

S	M	T	W	T	F	S
	1	2	3	4	5	6
7	8	9	10	11	12	13
14	15	16	17	18	19	20
21	22	23	24	25	26	27
28	29	30				

APRIL

15 MONDAY

16 TUESDAY

17 WEDNESDAY

18 THURSDAY

19 FRIDAY

20 SATURDAY

21 SUNDAY

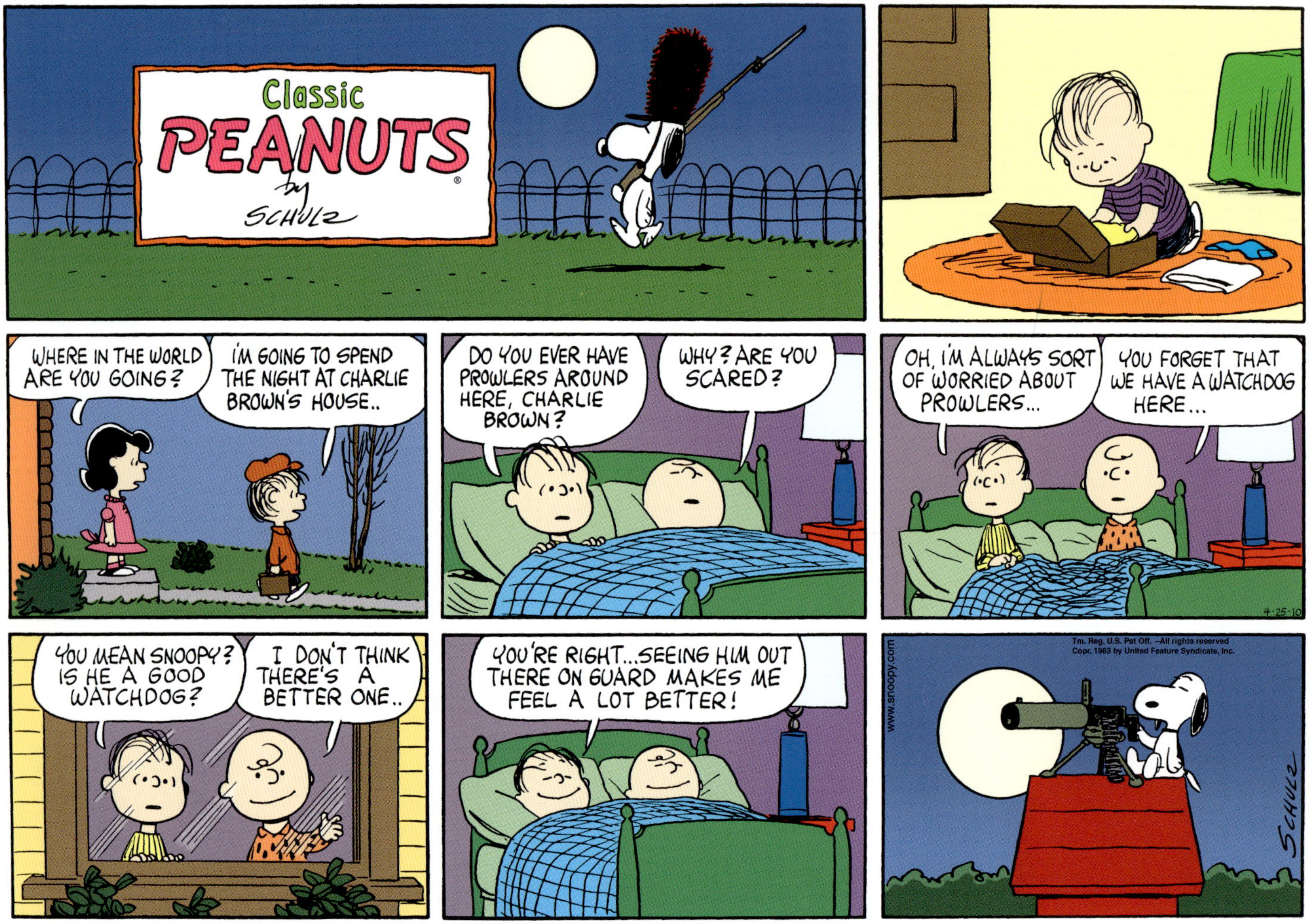
Classic PEANUTS by SCHULZ
WHERE IN THE WORLD ARE YOU GOING?
I'M GOING TO SPEND THE NIGHT AT CHARLIE BROWN'S HOUSE..
DO YOU EVER HAVE PROWLERS AROUND HERE, CHARLIE BROWN?
WHY? ARE YOU SCARED?
OH, I'M ALWAYS SORT OF WORRIED ABOUT PROWLERS...
YOU FORGET THAT WE HAVE A WATCHDOG HERE...
YOU MEAN SNOOPY? IS HE A GOOD WATCHDOG?
I DON'T THINK THERE'S A BETTER ONE..
YOU'RE RIGHT...SEEING HIM OUT THERE ON GUARD MAKES ME FEEL A LOT BETTER!
www.snoopy.com
Tm. Reg. U.S. Pat Off. –All rights reserved
Copr. 1963 by United Feature Syndicate, Inc.
SCHULZ

NOTES

April 2013

S	M	T	W	T	F	S
	1	2	3	4	5	6
7	8	9	10	11	12	13
14	15	16	17	18	19	20
21	22	23	24	25	26	27
28	29	30				

APRIL

22 MONDAY

Earth Day

23 TUESDAY

St. George's Day (UK)

24 WEDNESDAY

25 THURSDAY

Anzac Day (NZ, Australia)

26 FRIDAY

27 SATURDAY

28 SUNDAY

Classic
PEANUTS
by
SCHULZ
♪
SLURP
SLUP
SLURP
www.snoopy.com
5-2-10
Tm. Reg. U.S. Pat Off. –All rights reserved
Copr. 1963 by United Feature Syndicate, Inc.
WHERE? RIGHT HERE, THAT'S WHERE! RIGHT HERE ON PAGE THIRTY-ONE, SECTION THREE, RULE 6.12 !
I LOVE A GOOD RHUBARB
SCHULZ

NOTES

April 2013						
S	M	T	W	T	F	S
	1	2	3	4	5	6
7	8	9	10	11	12	13
14	15	16	17	18	19	20
21	22	23	24	25	26	27
28	29	30				

May 2013						
S	M	T	W	T	F	S
			1	2	3	4
5	6	7	8	9	10	11
12	13	14	15	16	17	18
19	20	21	22	23	24	25
26	27	28	29	30	31	

APRIL–MAY

29 MONDAY

30 TUESDAY

1 WEDNESDAY

2 THURSDAY

3 FRIDAY

Holy Friday (Orthodox)

4 SATURDAY

5 SUNDAY

Easter (Orthodox)

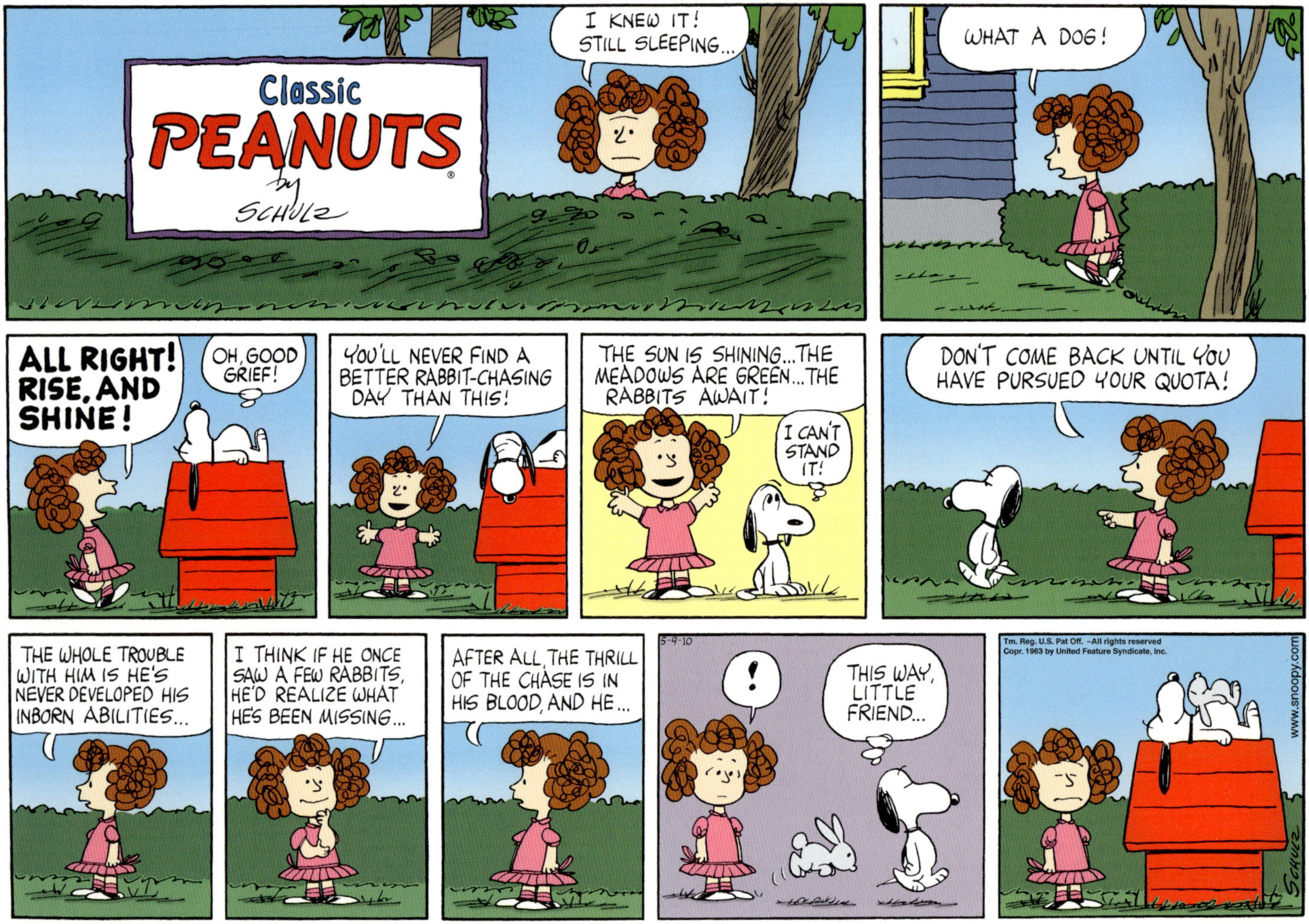
Classic PEANUTS by SCHULZ
I KNEW IT! STILL SLEEPING...
WHAT A DOG!
ALL RIGHT! RISE, AND SHINE!
OH, GOOD GRIEF!
YOU'LL NEVER FIND A BETTER RABBIT-CHASING DAY THAN THIS!
THE SUN IS SHINING...THE MEADOWS ARE GREEN...THE RABBITS AWAIT!
I CAN'T STAND IT!
DON'T COME BACK UNTIL YOU HAVE PURSUED YOUR QUOTA!
THE WHOLE TROUBLE WITH HIM IS HE'S NEVER DEVELOPED HIS INBORN ABILITIES...
I THINK IF HE ONCE SAW A FEW RABBITS, HE'D REALIZE WHAT HE'S BEEN MISSING...
AFTER ALL, THE THRILL OF THE CHASE IS IN HIS BLOOD, AND HE...
5-9-10
!
THIS WAY, LITTLE FRIEND...
Tm. Reg. U.S. Pat Off. –All rights reserved
Copr. 1963 by United Feature Syndicate, Inc.
www.snoopy.com
SCHULZ

NOTES

May 2013

S	M	T	W	T	F	S
			1	2	3	4
5	6	7	8	9	10	11
12	13	14	15	16	17	18
19	20	21	22	23	24	25
26	27	28	29	30	31	

MAY

6 MONDAY

Labour Day (Australia—QLD)

May Day (Australia—NT)

Early May Bank Holiday (Ireland, UK)

7 TUESDAY

8 WEDNESDAY

9 THURSDAY

10 FRIDAY

11 SATURDAY

12 SUNDAY

Mother's Day (USA, Australia, Canada, NZ)

Classic
PEANUTS
by
SCHULZ
HOLD STILL!
HOLD STILL, I SAY!
IS THIS A SCHOOL PROJECT, LUCY?
OF COURSE, IT IS, YOU BLOCKHEAD! WHY ELSE WOULD I BE CHASING A BUNCH OF STUPID BUTTERFLIES?!
5-16-10
Tm. Reg. U.S. Pat Off. –All rights reserved
Copr. 1963 by United Feature Syndicate, Inc.
HERE...I THINK MAYBE YOUR TEACHER WILL LIKE THESE..
PROMISE YOU'LL LET THEM GO AFTER YOU'VE STUDIED THEM, WILL YOU?
I JUST CAN'T BELIEVE THAT RACHEL CARSON WOULD EVER LET HERSELF GET SO UPSET!
www.snoopy.com
SCHULZ

NOTES

May 2013

S	M	T	W	T	F	S
			1	2	3	4
5	6	7	8	9	10	11
12	13	14	15	16	17	18
19	20	21	22	23	24	25
26	27	28	29	30	31	

MAY

13 MONDAY

14 TUESDAY

15 WEDNESDAY

16 THURSDAY

17 FRIDAY

18 SATURDAY

Armed Forces Day (USA)

19 SUNDAY

Classic
PEANUTS
by SCHULZ
EMPTY! AND I'M DYING OF THIRST!
5-23-10
www.snoopy.com
Tm. Reg. U.S. Pat Off. –All rights reserved
Copr. 1963 by United Feature Syndicate, Inc.
THAT'S ONE I'M GOING TO HAVE TO THINK ABOUT FOR AWHILE!
SCHULZ

NOTES

May 2013

S	M	T	W	T	F	S
			1	2	3	4
5	6	7	8	9	10	11
12	13	14	15	16	17	18
19	20	21	22	23	24	25
26	27	28	29	30	31	

20 MONDAY

Victoria Day (Canada)

21 TUESDAY

22 WEDNESDAY

23 THURSDAY

24 FRIDAY

25 SATURDAY

26 SUNDAY

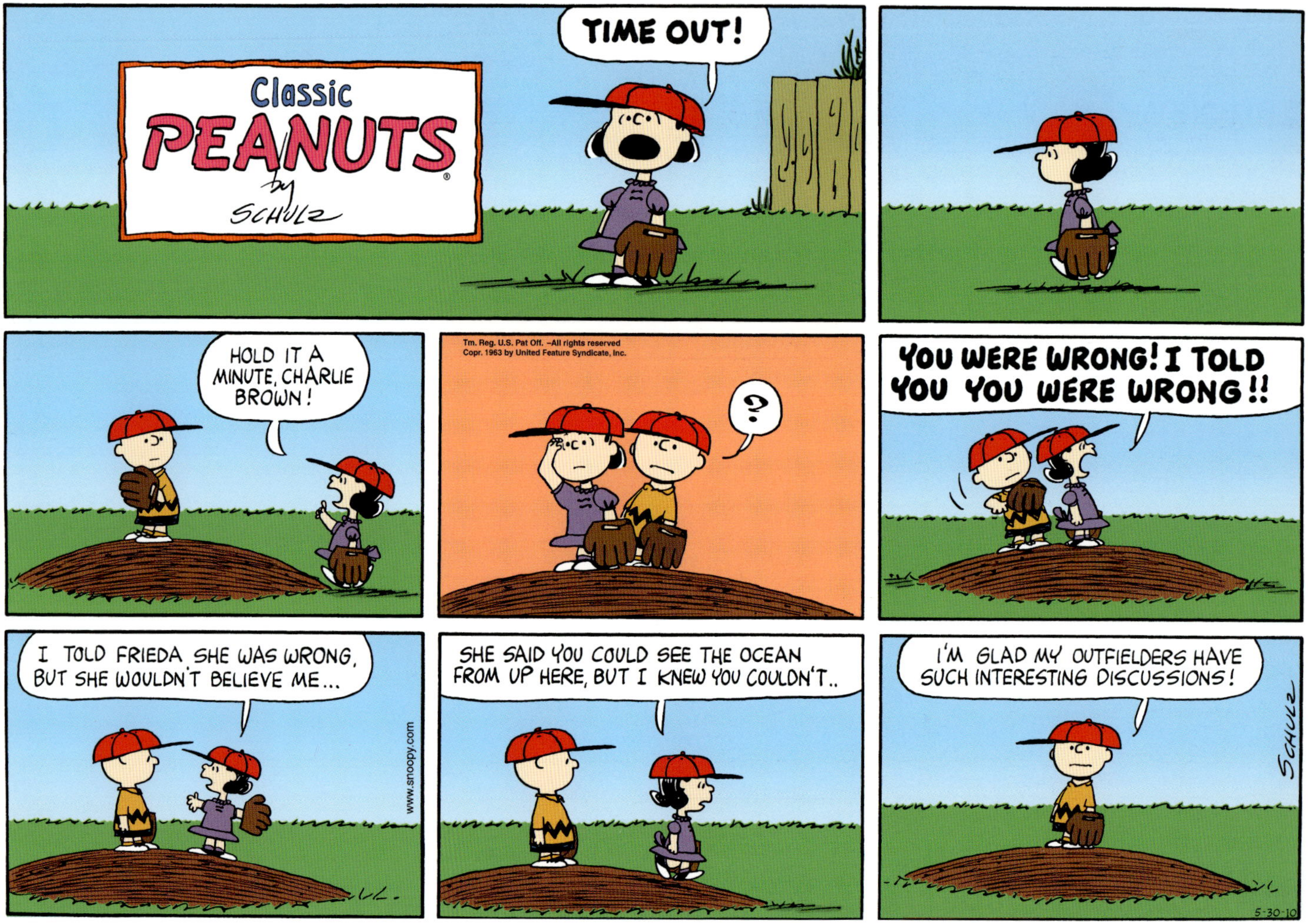

Classic
PEANUTS
by SCHULZ
TIME OUT!
HOLD IT A MINUTE, CHARLIE BROWN!
Tm. Reg. U.S. Pat Off. –All rights reserved
Copr. 1963 by United Feature Syndicate, Inc.
?
YOU WERE WRONG! I TOLD YOU YOU WERE WRONG!!
I TOLD FRIEDA SHE WAS WRONG, BUT SHE WOULDN'T BELIEVE ME...
www.snoopy.com
SHE SAID YOU COULD SEE THE OCEAN FROM UP HERE, BUT I KNEW YOU COULDN'T..
I'M GLAD MY OUTFIELDERS HAVE SUCH INTERESTING DISCUSSIONS!
SCHULZ
5-30-10

NOTES

May 2013

S	M	T	W	T	F	S
			1	2	3	4
5	6	7	8	9	10	11
12	13	14	15	16	17	18
19	20	21	22	23	24	25
26	27	28	29	30	31	

June 2013

S	M	T	W	T	F	S
						1
2	3	4	5	6	7	8
9	10	11	12	13	14	15
16	17	18	19	20	21	22
23	24	25	26	27	28	29
30						

MAY–JUNE

27 MONDAY

Memorial Day (USA)

Spring Bank Holiday (UK)

28 TUESDAY

29 WEDNESDAY

30 THURSDAY

31 FRIDAY

1 SATURDAY

2 SUNDAY

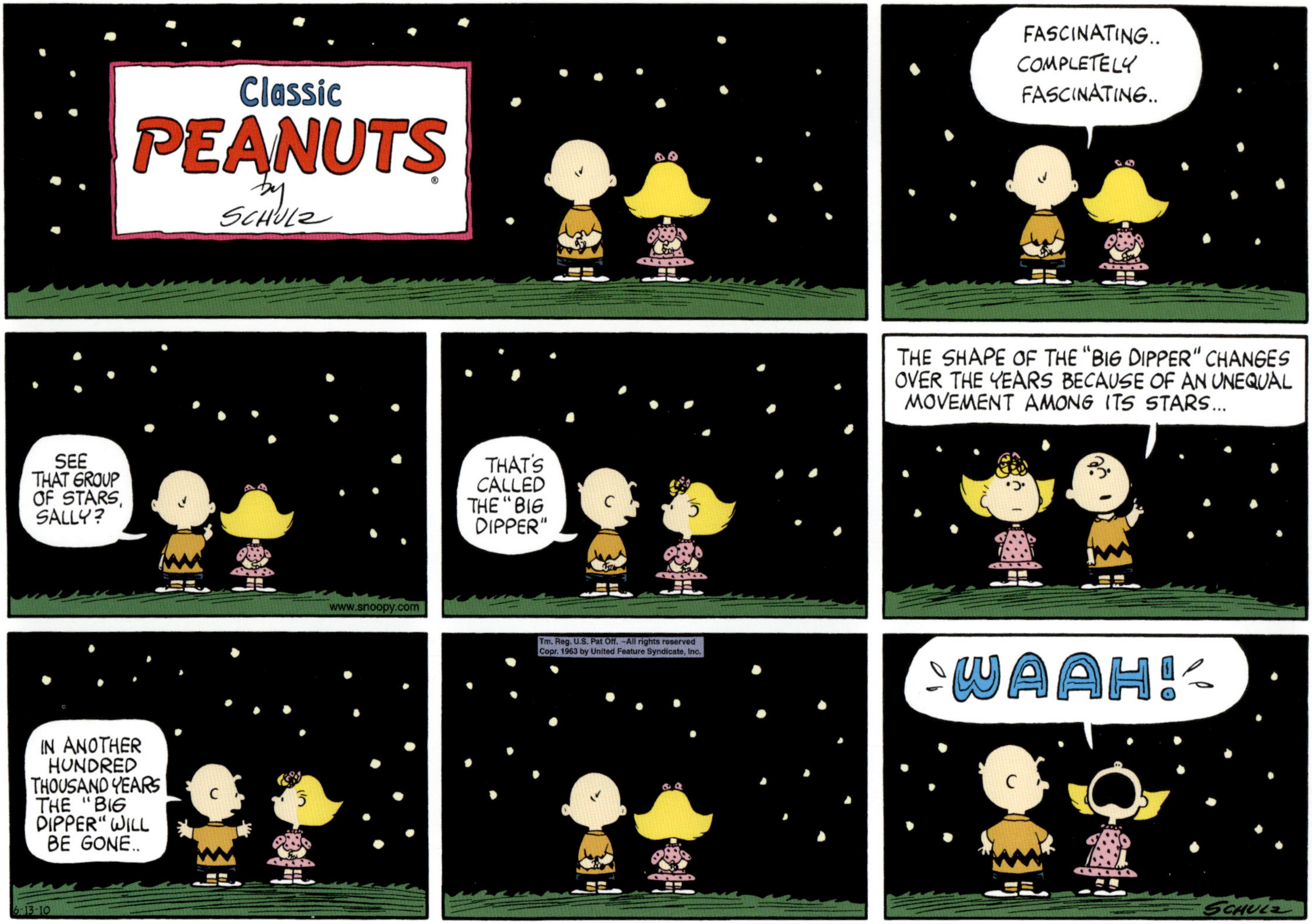
Classic PEANUTS by SCHULZ
FASCINATING.. COMPLETELY FASCINATING..
SEE THAT GROUP OF STARS, SALLY?
www.snoopy.com
THAT'S CALLED THE "BIG DIPPER"
THE SHAPE OF THE "BIG DIPPER" CHANGES OVER THE YEARS BECAUSE OF AN UNEQUAL MOVEMENT AMONG ITS STARS...
IN ANOTHER HUNDRED THOUSAND YEARS THE "BIG DIPPER" WILL BE GONE..
6-13-10
Tm. Reg. U.S. Pat Off. —All rights reserved Copr. 1963 by United Feature Syndicate, Inc.
WAAH!
SCHULZ

NOTES

June 2013

S	M	T	W	T	F	S
						1
2	3	4	5	6	7	8
9	10	11	12	13	14	15
16	17	18	19	20	21	22
23	24	25	26	27	28	29
30						

JUNE

3 MONDAY

Queen's Birthday (NZ)

Foundation Day (Australia—WA)

Spring Bank Holiday (Ireland)

4 TUESDAY

5 WEDNESDAY

6 THURSDAY

7 FRIDAY

8 SATURDAY

9 SUNDAY

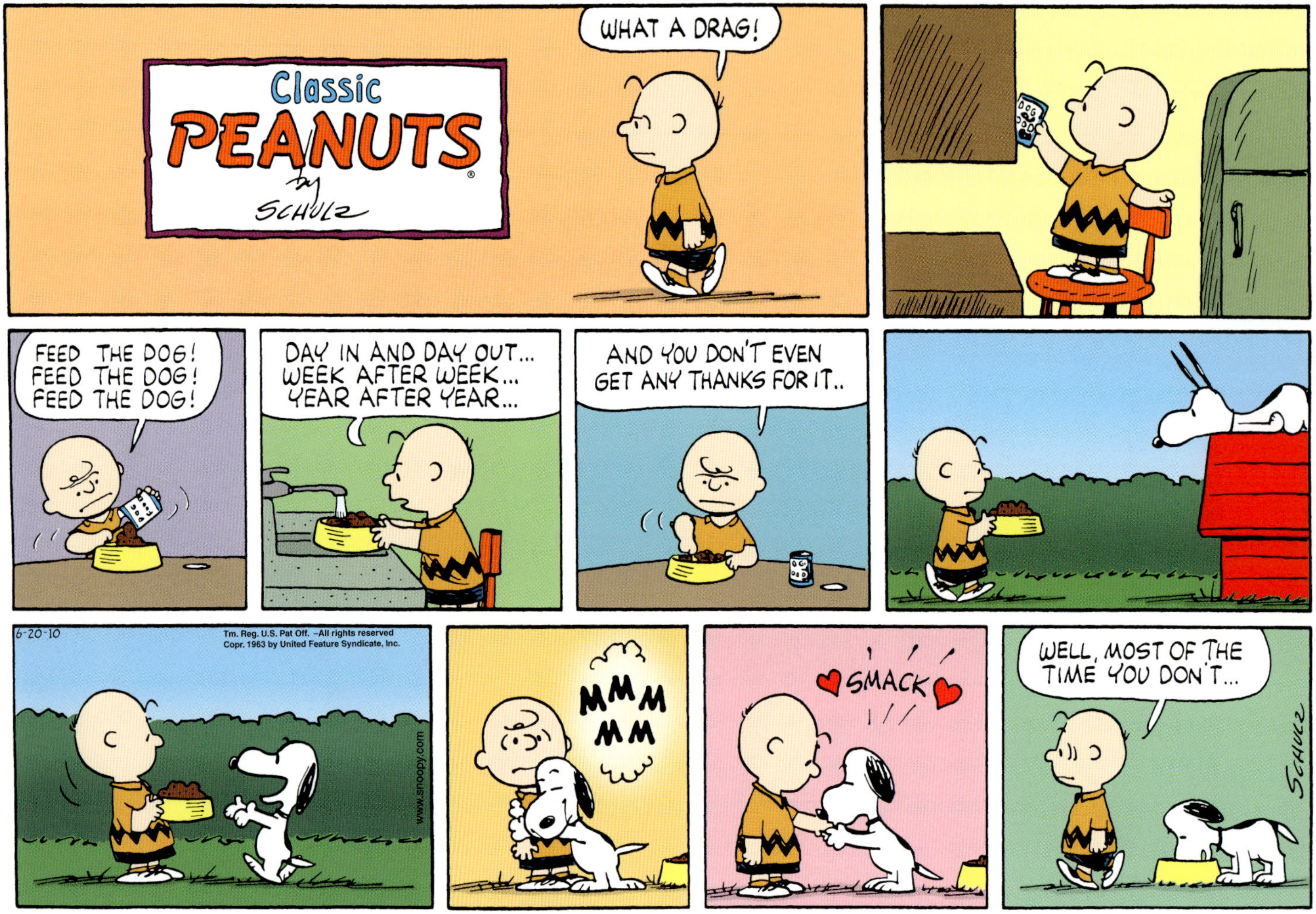
Classic PEANUTS by SCHULZ
WHAT A DRAG!
FEED THE DOG! FEED THE DOG! FEED THE DOG!
DAY IN AND DAY OUT... WEEK AFTER WEEK... YEAR AFTER YEAR...
AND YOU DON'T EVEN GET ANY THANKS FOR IT..
6-20-10
Tm. Reg. U.S. Pat Off. –All rights reserved
Copr. 1963 by United Feature Syndicate, Inc.
www.snoopy.com
MMM MM
SMACK
WELL, MOST OF THE TIME YOU DON'T...
SCHULZ

NOTES

June 2013

S	M	T	W	T	F	S
						1
2	3	4	5	6	7	8
9	10	11	12	13	14	15
16	17	18	19	20	21	22
23	24	25	26	27	28	29
30						

JUNE

10 MONDAY

Queen's Birthday (Australia—except WA)

11 TUESDAY

12 WEDNESDAY

13 THURSDAY

14 FRIDAY

Flag Day (USA)

15 SATURDAY

16 SUNDAY

Father's Day (USA, Canada, Ireland, UK)

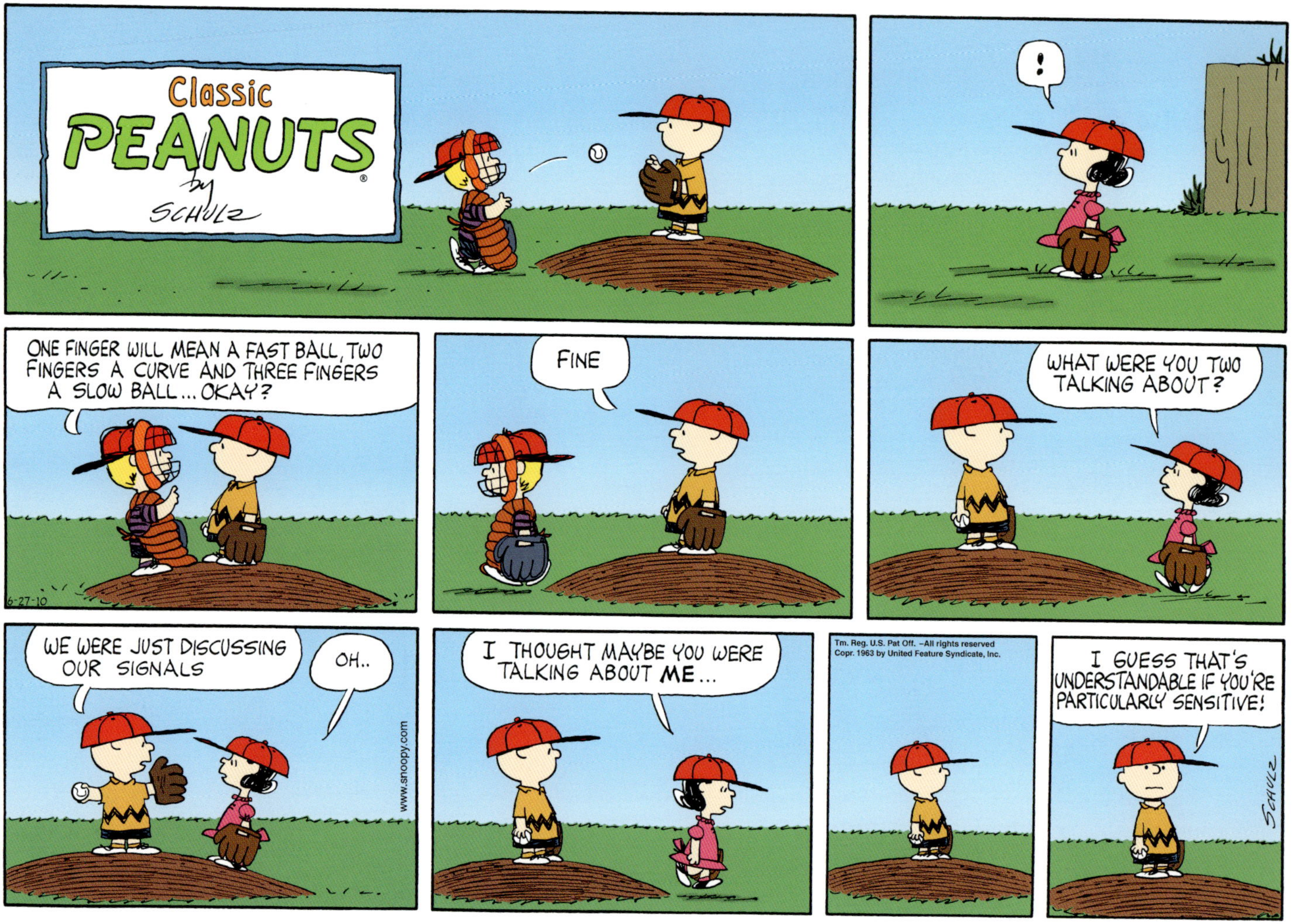
Classic
PEANUTS
by SCHULZ
!
ONE FINGER WILL MEAN A FAST BALL, TWO FINGERS A CURVE AND THREE FINGERS A SLOW BALL... OKAY?
6-27-10
FINE
WHAT WERE YOU TWO TALKING ABOUT?
WE WERE JUST DISCUSSING OUR SIGNALS
OH..
www.snoopy.com
I THOUGHT MAYBE YOU WERE TALKING ABOUT **ME**...
Tm. Reg. U.S. Pat Off. –All rights reserved
Copr. 1963 by United Feature Syndicate, Inc.
I GUESS THAT'S UNDERSTANDABLE IF YOU'RE PARTICULARLY SENSITIVE!
SCHULZ

NOTES

June 2013

S	M	T	W	T	F	S
						1
2	3	4	5	6	7	8
9	10	11	12	13	14	15
16	17	18	19	20	21	22
23	24	25	26	27	28	29
30						

JUNE

17 MONDAY

18 TUESDAY

19 WEDNESDAY

20 THURSDAY

21 FRIDAY

22 SATURDAY

23 SUNDAY

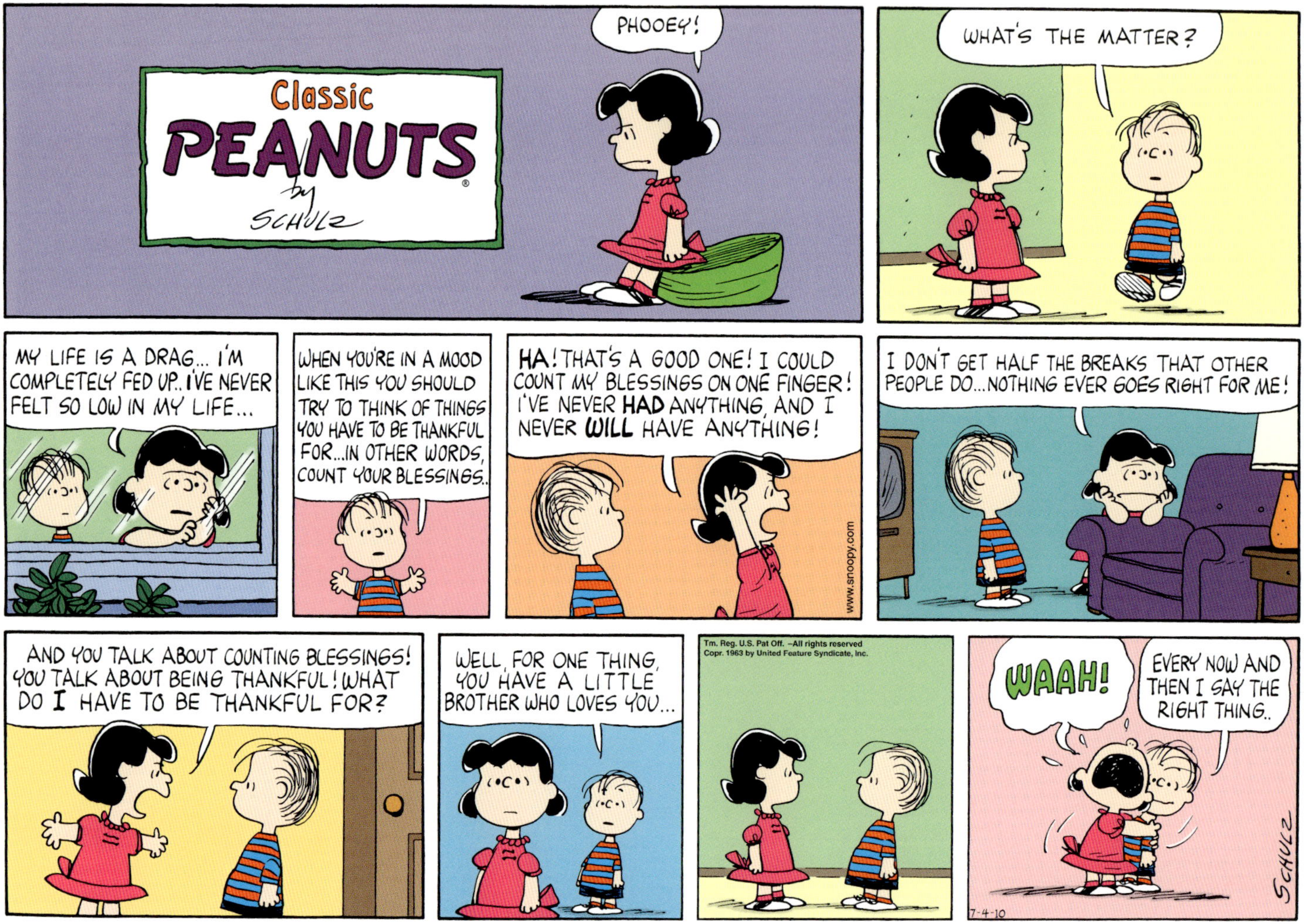
Classic
PEANUTS
by SCHULZ
PHOOEY!
WHAT'S THE MATTER?
MY LIFE IS A DRAG... I'M COMPLETELY FED UP.. I'VE NEVER FELT SO LOW IN MY LIFE...
WHEN YOU'RE IN A MOOD LIKE THIS YOU SHOULD TRY TO THINK OF THINGS YOU HAVE TO BE THANKFUL FOR...IN OTHER WORDS, COUNT YOUR BLESSINGS..
HA! THAT'S A GOOD ONE! I COULD COUNT MY BLESSINGS ON ONE FINGER! I'VE NEVER HAD ANYTHING, AND I NEVER WILL HAVE ANYTHING!
www.snoopy.com
I DON'T GET HALF THE BREAKS THAT OTHER PEOPLE DO...NOTHING EVER GOES RIGHT FOR ME!
AND YOU TALK ABOUT COUNTING BLESSINGS! YOU TALK ABOUT BEING THANKFUL! WHAT DO I HAVE TO BE THANKFUL FOR?
WELL, FOR ONE THING, YOU HAVE A LITTLE BROTHER WHO LOVES YOU...
Tm. Reg. U.S. Pat Off. –All rights reserved
Copr. 1963 by United Feature Syndicate, Inc.
WAAH!
EVERY NOW AND THEN I SAY THE RIGHT THING..
7-4-10
SCHULZ

NOTES

June 2013

S	M	T	W	T	F	S
						1
2	3	4	5	6	7	8
9	10	11	12	13	14	15
16	17	18	19	20	21	22
23	24	25	26	27	28	29
30						

24 MONDAY

25 TUESDAY

26 WEDNESDAY

27 THURSDAY

28 FRIDAY

29 SATURDAY

30 SUNDAY

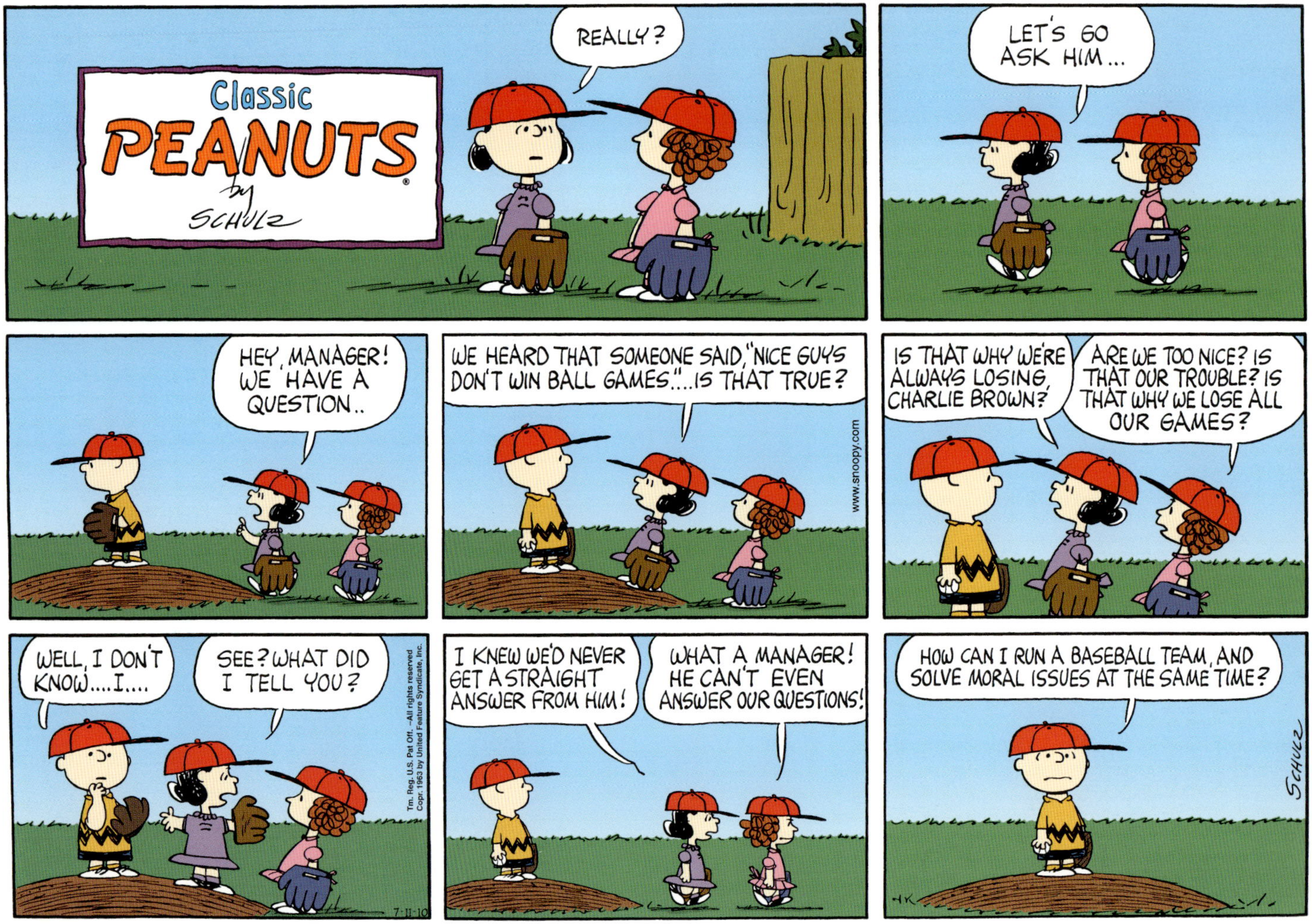
Classic PEANUTS by SCHULZ
REALLY?
LET'S GO ASK HIM...
HEY, MANAGER! WE HAVE A QUESTION..
WE HEARD THAT SOMEONE SAID, "NICE GUYS DON'T WIN BALL GAMES."...IS THAT TRUE?
www.snoopy.com
IS THAT WHY WE'RE ALWAYS LOSING, CHARLIE BROWN?
ARE WE TOO NICE? IS THAT OUR TROUBLE? IS THAT WHY WE LOSE ALL OUR GAMES?
WELL, I DON'T KNOW....I....
SEE? WHAT DID I TELL YOU?
Tm. Reg. U.S. Pat Off.—All rights reserved
Copr. 1963 by United Feature Syndicate, Inc.
7-11-10
I KNEW WE'D NEVER GET A STRAIGHT ANSWER FROM HIM!
WHAT A MANAGER! HE CAN'T EVEN ANSWER OUR QUESTIONS!
HOW CAN I RUN A BASEBALL TEAM, AND SOLVE MORAL ISSUES AT THE SAME TIME?
SCHULZ

NOTES

July 2013

S	M	T	W	T	F	S
	1	2	3	4	5	6
7	8	9	10	11	12	13
14	15	16	17	18	19	20
21	22	23	24	25	26	27
28	29	30	31			

JULY

1 MONDAY

Canada Day

2 TUESDAY

3 WEDNESDAY

4 THURSDAY

Independence Day (USA)

5 FRIDAY

6 SATURDAY

7 SUNDAY

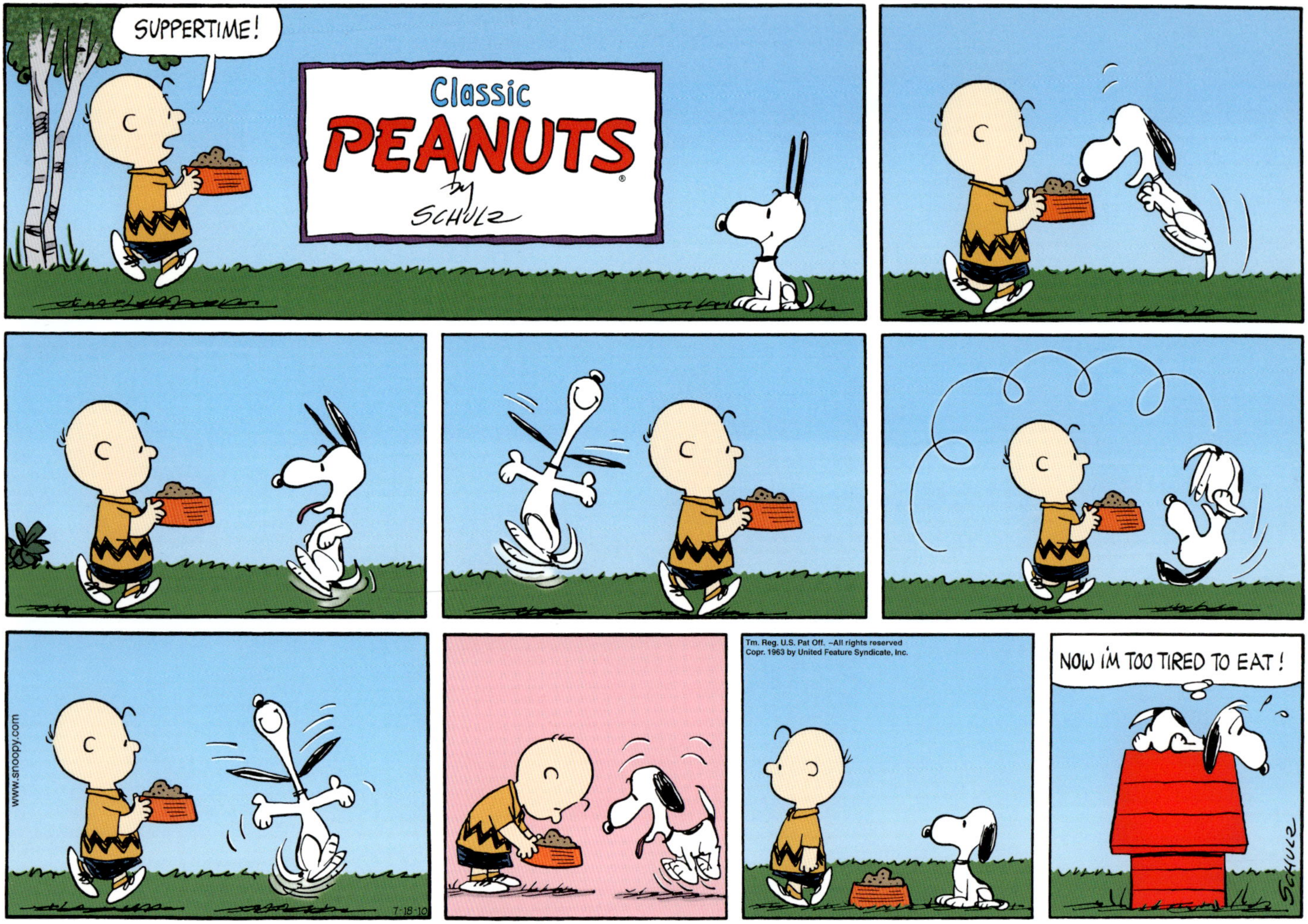
SUPPERTIME!
Classic
PEANUTS
by SCHULZ
www.snoopy.com
7-18-10
Tm. Reg. U.S. Pat Off. –All rights reserved
Copr. 1963 by United Feature Syndicate, Inc.
NOW I'M TOO TIRED TO EAT!
SCHULZ

NOTES

July 2013

S	M	T	W	T	F	S
	1	2	3	4	5	6
7	8	9	10	11	12	13
14	15	16	17	18	19	20
21	22	23	24	25	26	27
28	29	30	31			

JULY

8 MONDAY

9 TUESDAY

Ramadan

10 WEDNESDAY

11 THURSDAY

12 FRIDAY

13 SATURDAY

14 SUNDAY

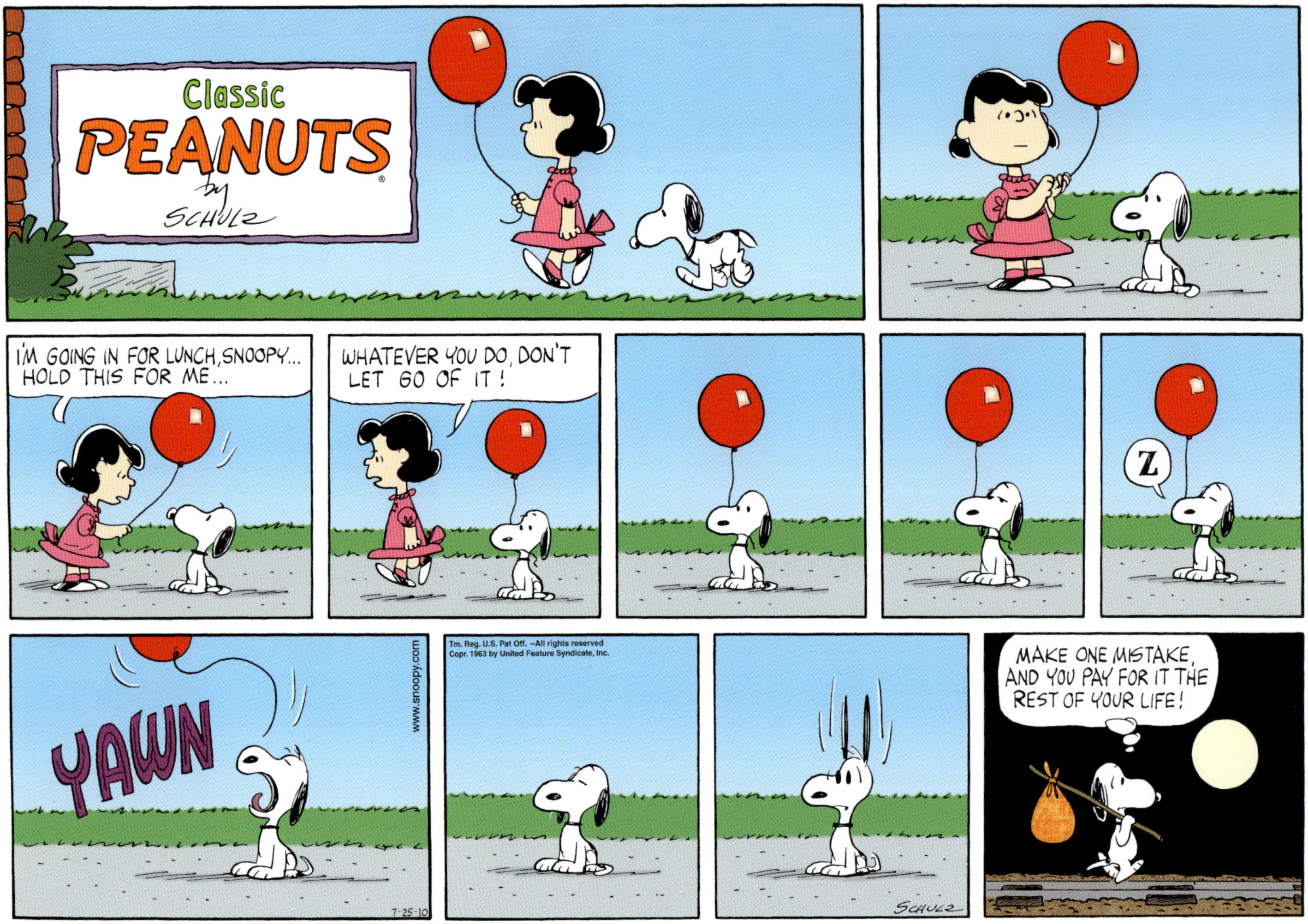
Classic PEANUTS by SCHULZ
I'M GOING IN FOR LUNCH, SNOOPY... HOLD THIS FOR ME...
WHATEVER YOU DO, DON'T LET GO OF IT!
Z
YAWN
www.snoopy.com
7-25-10
Tm. Reg. U.S. Pat Off. —All rights reserved
Copr. 1963 by United Feature Syndicate, Inc.
SCHULZ
MAKE ONE MISTAKE, AND YOU PAY FOR IT THE REST OF YOUR LIFE!

NOTES

July 2013

S	M	T	W	T	F	S
	1	2	3	4	5	6
7	8	9	10	11	12	13
14	15	16	17	18	19	20
21	22	23	24	25	26	27
28	29	30	31			

JULY

15 MONDAY

16 TUESDAY

17 WEDNESDAY

18 THURSDAY

19 FRIDAY

20 SATURDAY

21 SUNDAY

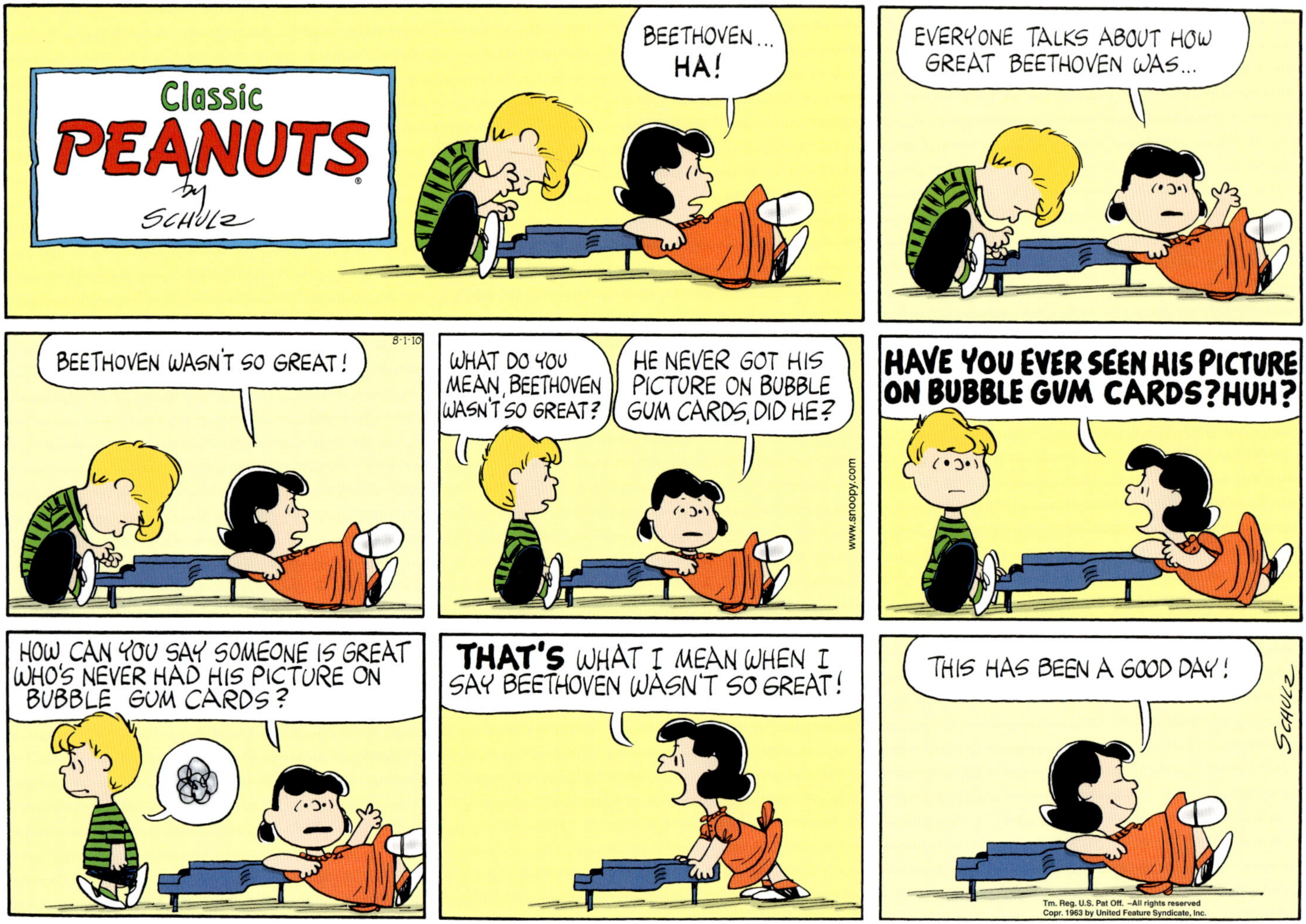
Classic PEANUTS by SCHULZ
BEETHOVEN... HA!
EVERYONE TALKS ABOUT HOW GREAT BEETHOVEN WAS...
BEETHOVEN WASN'T SO GREAT!
8-1-10
WHAT DO YOU MEAN, BEETHOVEN WASN'T SO GREAT?
HE NEVER GOT HIS PICTURE ON BUBBLE GUM CARDS, DID HE?
www.snoopy.com
HAVE YOU EVER SEEN HIS PICTURE ON BUBBLE GUM CARDS? HUH?
HOW CAN YOU SAY SOMEONE IS GREAT WHO'S NEVER HAD HIS PICTURE ON BUBBLE GUM CARDS?
THAT'S WHAT I MEAN WHEN I SAY BEETHOVEN WASN'T SO GREAT!
THIS HAS BEEN A GOOD DAY!
SCHULZ
Tm. Reg. U.S. Pat Off. –All rights reserved
Copr. 1963 by United Feature Syndicate, Inc.

NOTES

July 2013

S	M	T	W	T	F	S
	1	2	3	4	5	6
7	8	9	10	11	12	13
14	15	16	17	18	19	20
21	22	23	24	25	26	27
28	29	30	31			

JULY

22 MONDAY

23 TUESDAY

24 WEDNESDAY

25 THURSDAY

26 FRIDAY

27 SATURDAY

28 SUNDAY

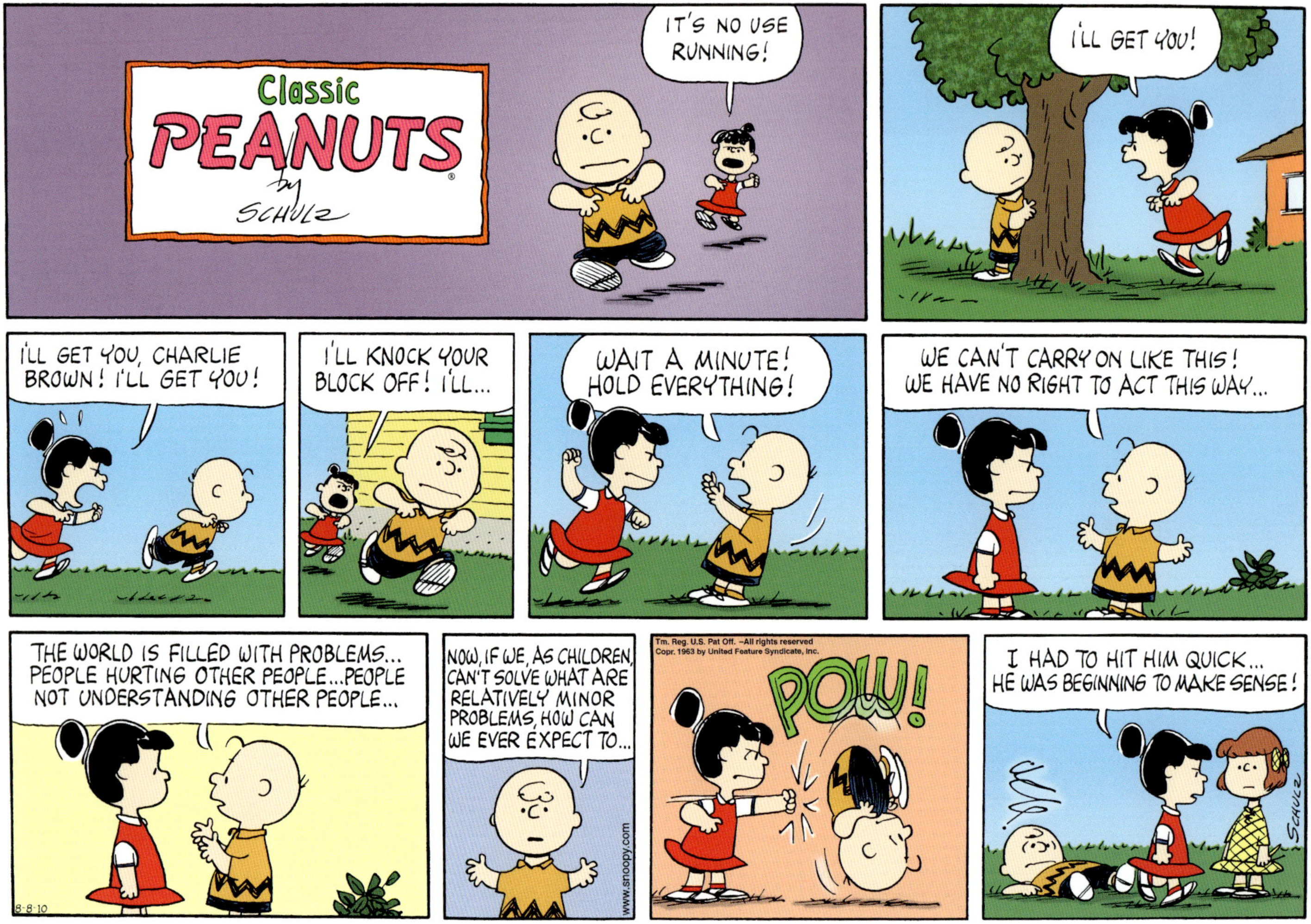
Classic
PEANUTS
by SCHULZ
IT'S NO USE RUNNING!
I'LL GET YOU!
I'LL GET YOU, CHARLIE BROWN! I'LL GET YOU!
I'LL KNOCK YOUR BLOCK OFF! I'LL...
WAIT A MINUTE! HOLD EVERYTHING!
WE CAN'T CARRY ON LIKE THIS! WE HAVE NO RIGHT TO ACT THIS WAY...
THE WORLD IS FILLED WITH PROBLEMS... PEOPLE HURTING OTHER PEOPLE...PEOPLE NOT UNDERSTANDING OTHER PEOPLE...
8-8-10
NOW, IF WE, AS CHILDREN, CAN'T SOLVE WHAT ARE RELATIVELY MINOR PROBLEMS, HOW CAN WE EVER EXPECT TO...
www.snoopy.com
Tm. Reg. U.S. Pat Off. –All rights reserved
Copr. 1963 by United Feature Syndicate, Inc.
POW!
I HAD TO HIT HIM QUICK... HE WAS BEGINNING TO MAKE SENSE!
SCHULZ

NOTES

July 2013

S	M	T	W	T	F	S
	1	2	3	4	5	6
7	8	9	10	11	12	13
14	15	16	17	18	19	20
21	22	23	24	25	26	27
28	29	30	31			

August 2013

S	M	T	W	T	F	S
				1	2	3
4	5	6	7	8	9	10
11	12	13	14	15	16	17
18	19	20	21	22	23	24
25	26	27	28	29	30	31

JULY–AUGUST

29 MONDAY

30 TUESDAY

31 WEDNESDAY

1 THURSDAY

2 FRIDAY

3 SATURDAY

4 SUNDAY

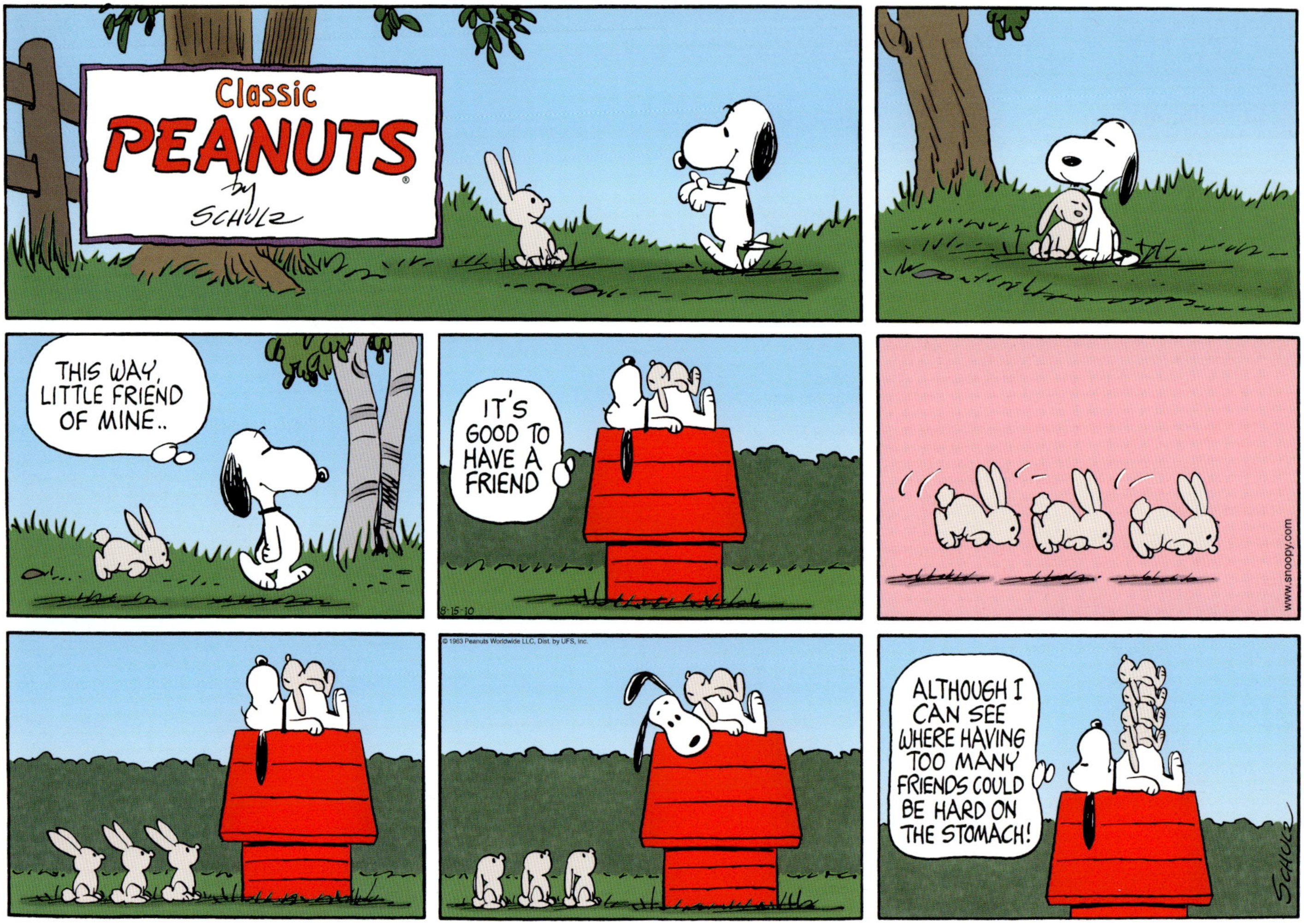
Classic
PEANUTS
by
SCHULZ
THIS WAY, LITTLE FRIEND OF MINE..
IT'S GOOD TO HAVE A FRIEND
8-15-10
www.snoopy.com
© 1963 Peanuts Worldwide LLC, Dist. by UFS, Inc.
ALTHOUGH I CAN SEE WHERE HAVING TOO MANY FRIENDS COULD BE HARD ON THE STOMACH!
SCHULZ

NOTES

August 2013

S	M	T	W	T	F	S
				1	2	3
4	5	6	7	8	9	10
11	12	13	14	15	16	17
18	19	20	21	22	23	24
25	26	27	28	29	30	31

AUGUST

5 MONDAY

Summer Bank Holiday
(Ireland, UK—Scotland, Australia—NSW)

Picnic Day (Australia—NT)

6 TUESDAY

7 WEDNESDAY

8 THURSDAY

Eid al-Fitr

9 FRIDAY

10 SATURDAY

11 SUNDAY

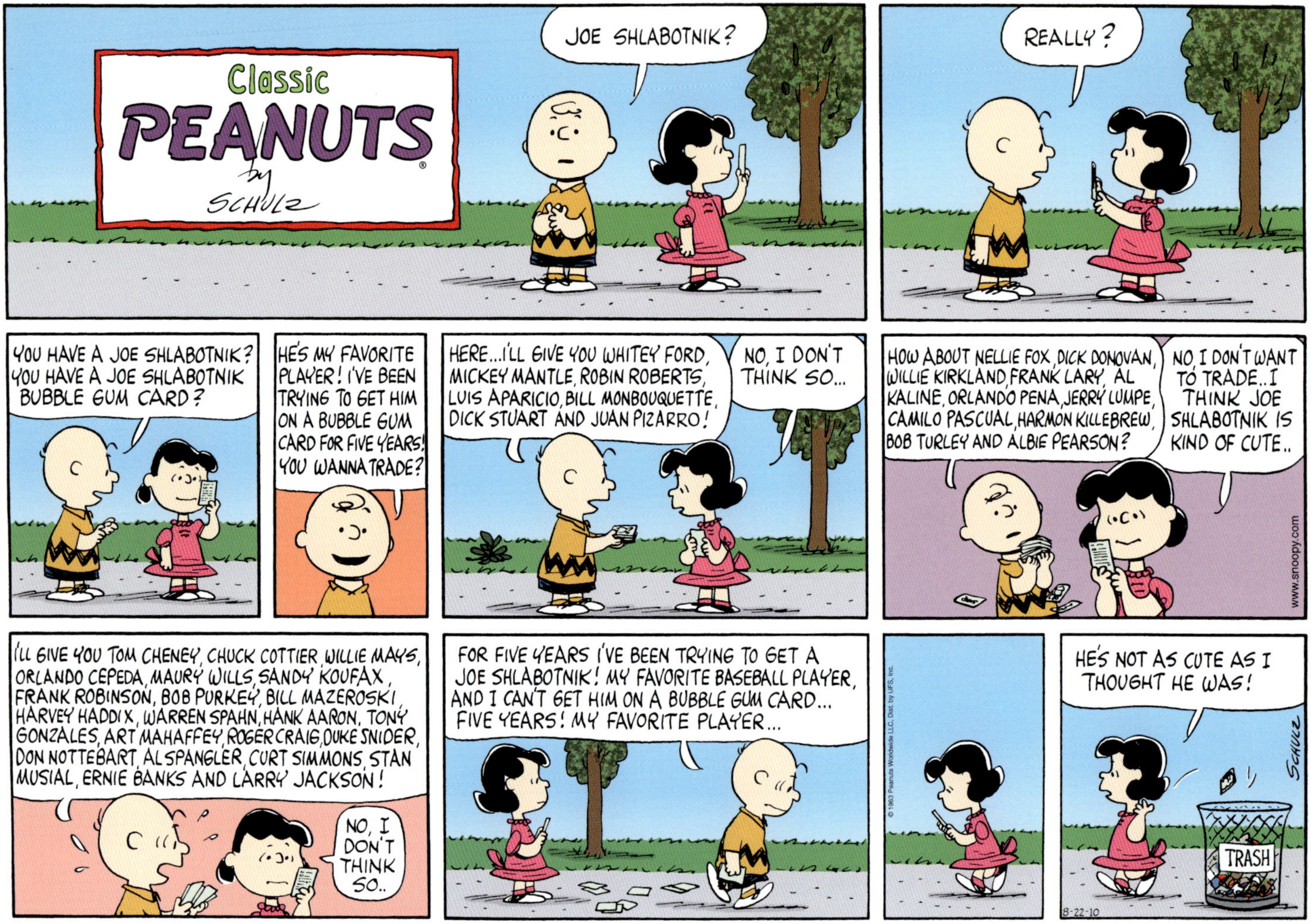
Classic PEANUTS by SCHULZ
JOE SHLABOTNIK?
REALLY?
YOU HAVE A JOE SHLABOTNIK? YOU HAVE A JOE SHLABOTNIK BUBBLE GUM CARD?
HE'S MY FAVORITE PLAYER! I'VE BEEN TRYING TO GET HIM ON A BUBBLE GUM CARD FOR FIVE YEARS! YOU WANNA TRADE?
HERE...I'LL GIVE YOU WHITEY FORD, MICKEY MANTLE, ROBIN ROBERTS, LUIS APARICIO, BILL MONBOUQUETTE, DICK STUART AND JUAN PIZARRO!
NO, I DON'T THINK SO...
HOW ABOUT NELLIE FOX, DICK DONOVAN, WILLIE KIRKLAND, FRANK LARY, AL KALINE, ORLANDO PENA, JERRY LUMPE, CAMILO PASCUAL, HARMON KILLEBREW, BOB TURLEY AND ALBIE PEARSON?
NO, I DON'T WANT TO TRADE..I THINK JOE SHLABOTNIK IS KIND OF CUTE..
www.snoopy.com
I'LL GIVE YOU TOM CHENEY, CHUCK COTTIER, WILLIE MAYS, ORLANDO CEPEDA, MAURY WILLS, SANDY KOUFAX, FRANK ROBINSON, BOB PURKEY, BILL MAZEROSKI, HARVEY HADDIX, WARREN SPAHN, HANK AARON, TONY GONZALES, ART MAHAFFEY, ROGER CRAIG, DUKE SNIDER, DON NOTTEBART, AL SPANGLER, CURT SIMMONS, STAN MUSIAL, ERNIE BANKS AND LARRY JACKSON!
NO, I DON'T THINK SO..
FOR FIVE YEARS I'VE BEEN TRYING TO GET A JOE SHLABOTNIK! MY FAVORITE BASEBALL PLAYER, AND I CAN'T GET HIM ON A BUBBLE GUM CARD... FIVE YEARS! MY FAVORITE PLAYER...
© 1963 Peanuts Worldwide LLC. Dist. by UFS, Inc.
HE'S NOT AS CUTE AS I THOUGHT HE WAS!
TRASH
SCHULZ
8-22-10

NOTES

August 2013

S	M	T	W	T	F	S
				1	2	3
4	5	6	7	8	9	10
11	12	13	14	15	16	17
18	19	20	21	22	23	24
25	26	27	28	29	30	31

AUGUST

12 MONDAY

13 TUESDAY

14 WEDNESDAY

15 THURSDAY

16 FRIDAY

17 SATURDAY

18 SUNDAY

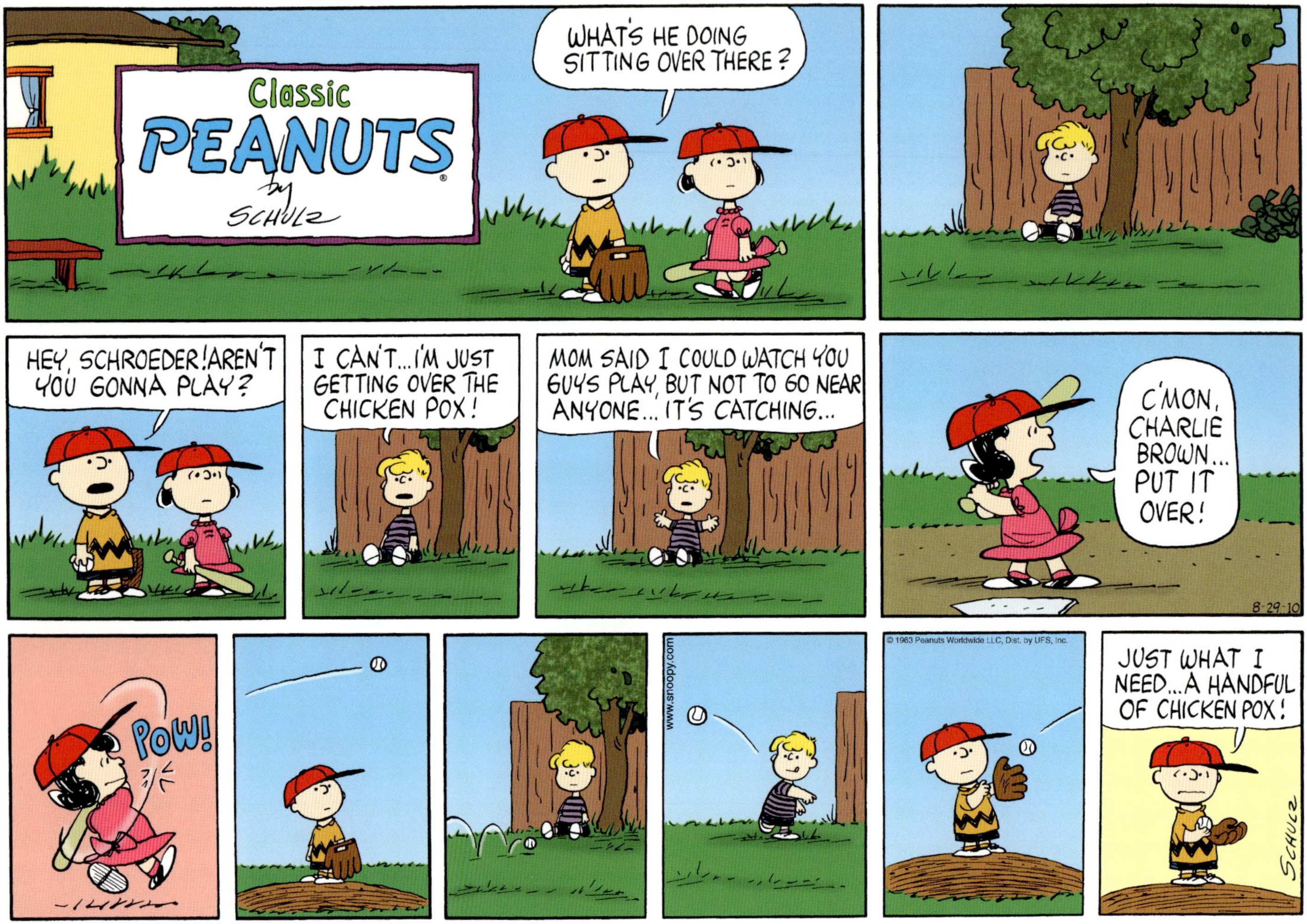
Classic PEANUTS by SCHULZ
WHAT'S HE DOING SITTING OVER THERE?
HEY, SCHROEDER! AREN'T YOU GONNA PLAY?
I CAN'T...I'M JUST GETTING OVER THE CHICKEN POX!
MOM SAID I COULD WATCH YOU GUYS PLAY, BUT NOT TO GO NEAR ANYONE... IT'S CATCHING...
C'MON, CHARLIE BROWN... PUT IT OVER!
8-29-10
POW!
www.snoopy.com
© 1963 Peanuts Worldwide LLC, Dist. by UFS, Inc.
JUST WHAT I NEED...A HANDFUL OF CHICKEN POX!
SCHULZ

NOTES

August 2013

S	M	T	W	T	F	S
				1	2	3
4	5	6	7	8	9	10
11	12	13	14	15	16	17
18	19	20	21	22	23	24
25	26	27	28	29	30	31

AUGUST

19 MONDAY

20 TUESDAY

21 WEDNESDAY

22 THURSDAY

23 FRIDAY

24 SATURDAY

25 SUNDAY

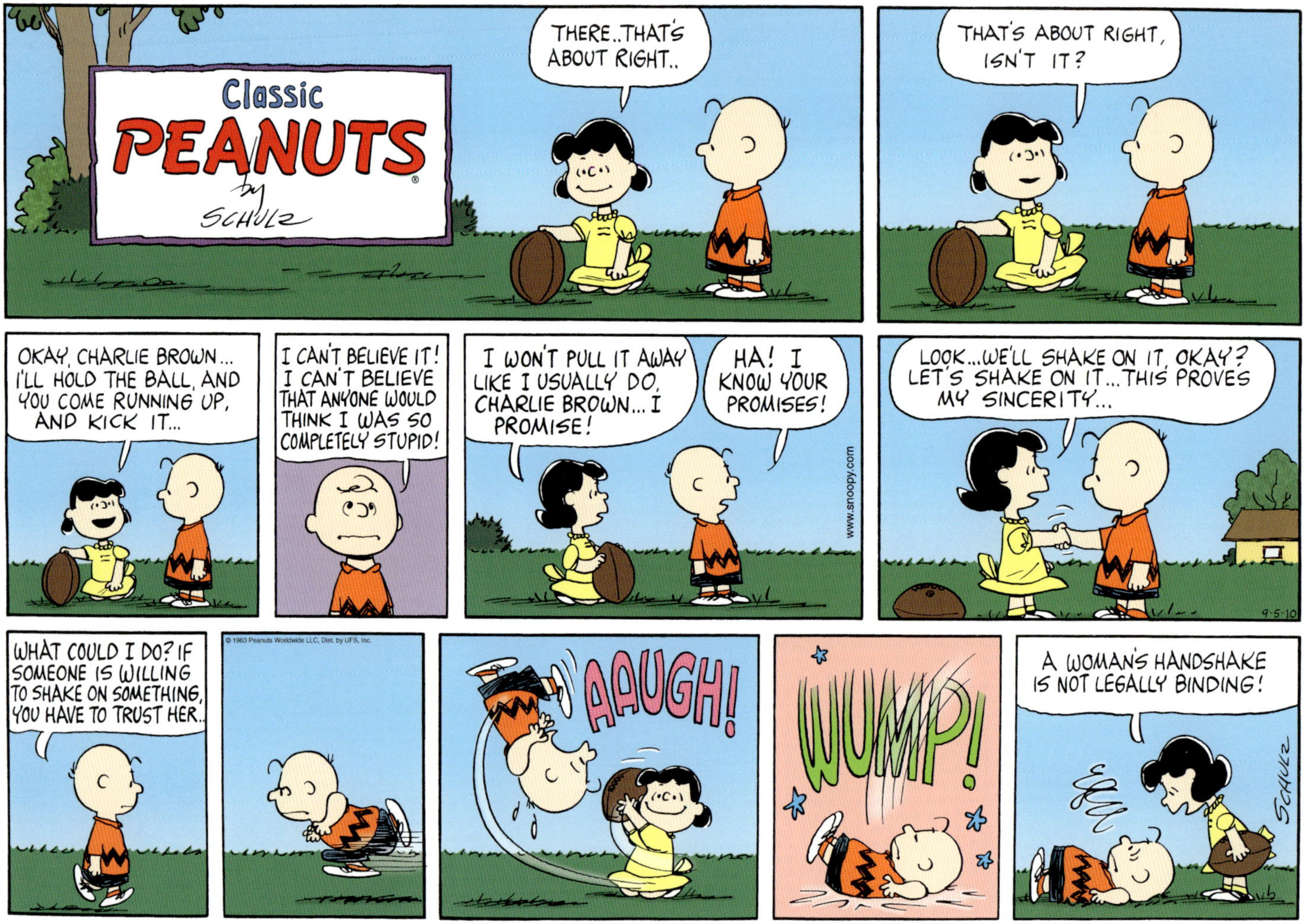
Classic
PEANUTS
by SCHULZ
THERE..THAT'S ABOUT RIGHT..
THAT'S ABOUT RIGHT, ISN'T IT?
OKAY, CHARLIE BROWN... I'LL HOLD THE BALL, AND YOU COME RUNNING UP, AND KICK IT...
I CAN'T BELIEVE IT! I CAN'T BELIEVE THAT ANYONE WOULD THINK I WAS SO COMPLETELY STUPID!
I WON'T PULL IT AWAY LIKE I USUALLY DO, CHARLIE BROWN... I PROMISE!
HA! I KNOW YOUR PROMISES!
www.snoopy.com
LOOK...WE'LL SHAKE ON IT, OKAY? LET'S SHAKE ON IT... THIS PROVES MY SINCERITY...
9-5-10
WHAT COULD I DO? IF SOMEONE IS WILLING TO SHAKE ON SOMETHING, YOU HAVE TO TRUST HER..
© 1963 Peanuts Worldwide LLC, Dist. by UFS, Inc.
AAUGH!
WUMP!
A WOMAN'S HANDSHAKE IS NOT LEGALLY BINDING!
SCHULZ

NOTES

August 2013

S	M	T	W	T	F	S
				1	2	3
4	5	6	7	8	9	10
11	12	13	14	15	16	17
18	19	20	21	22	23	24
25	26	27	28	29	30	31

September 2013

S	M	T	W	T	F	S
1	2	3	4	5	6	7
8	9	10	11	12	13	14
15	16	17	18	19	20	21
22	23	24	25	26	27	28
29	30					

AUGUST–SEPTEMBER

26 MONDAY

Summer Bank Holiday (UK—except Scotland)

27 TUESDAY

28 WEDNESDAY

29 THURSDAY

30 FRIDAY

31 SATURDAY

1 SUNDAY

Father's Day (Australia, NZ)

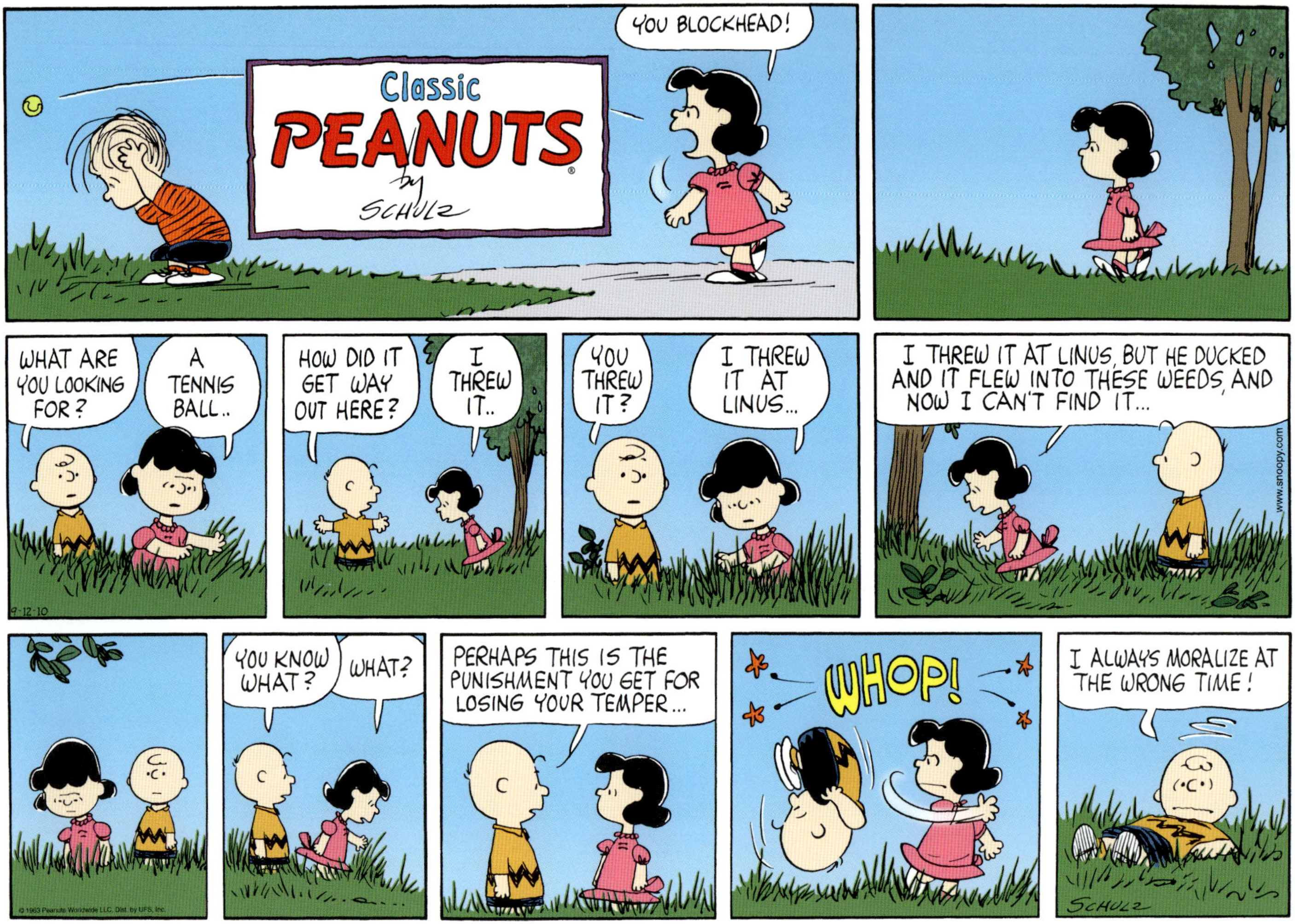
Classic PEANUTS by SCHULZ
YOU BLOCKHEAD!
WHAT ARE YOU LOOKING FOR?
A TENNIS BALL..
HOW DID IT GET WAY OUT HERE?
I THREW IT..
YOU THREW IT?
I THREW IT AT LINUS...
I THREW IT AT LINUS, BUT HE DUCKED AND IT FLEW INTO THESE WEEDS, AND NOW I CAN'T FIND IT...
www.snoopy.com
9-12-10
YOU KNOW WHAT?
WHAT?
PERHAPS THIS IS THE PUNISHMENT YOU GET FOR LOSING YOUR TEMPER...
WHOP!
I ALWAYS MORALIZE AT THE WRONG TIME!
SCHULZ
© 1963 Peanuts Worldwide LLC. Dist. by UFS, Inc.

NOTES

September 2013

S	M	T	W	T	F	S
1	2	3	4	5	6	7
8	9	10	11	12	13	14
15	16	17	18	19	20	21
22	23	24	25	26	27	28
29	30					

SEPTEMBER

2 MONDAY

Labor Day (USA, Canada)

3 TUESDAY

4 WEDNESDAY

5 THURSDAY

*Rosh Hashanah**

6 FRIDAY

Rosh Hashanah ends

7 SATURDAY

8 SUNDAY

**Begins at sundown the previous day*

Classic
PEANUTS
by
SCHULZ
MAILMAN!
9-19-10
OH, I SEE IT CAME...
THIS IS FROM YOU?
UH HUH.. GO AHEAD, AND READ IT...
www.snoopy.com
"Best wishes to you and yours for a Happy Holiday Season ~"
© 1963 Peanuts Worldwide LLC. Dist. by UFS, Inc.
THIS YEAR I MADE UP MY MIND I WAS GOING TO GET THEM OUT EARLY!
SCHULZ

NOTES

September 2013

S	M	T	W	T	F	S
1	2	3	4	5	6	7
8	9	10	11	12	13	14
15	16	17	18	19	20	21
22	23	24	25	26	27	28
29	30					

SEPTEMBER

9 MONDAY

10 TUESDAY

11 WEDNESDAY

12 THURSDAY

13 FRIDAY

14 SATURDAY

*Yom Kippur**

15 SUNDAY

**Begins at sundown the previous day*

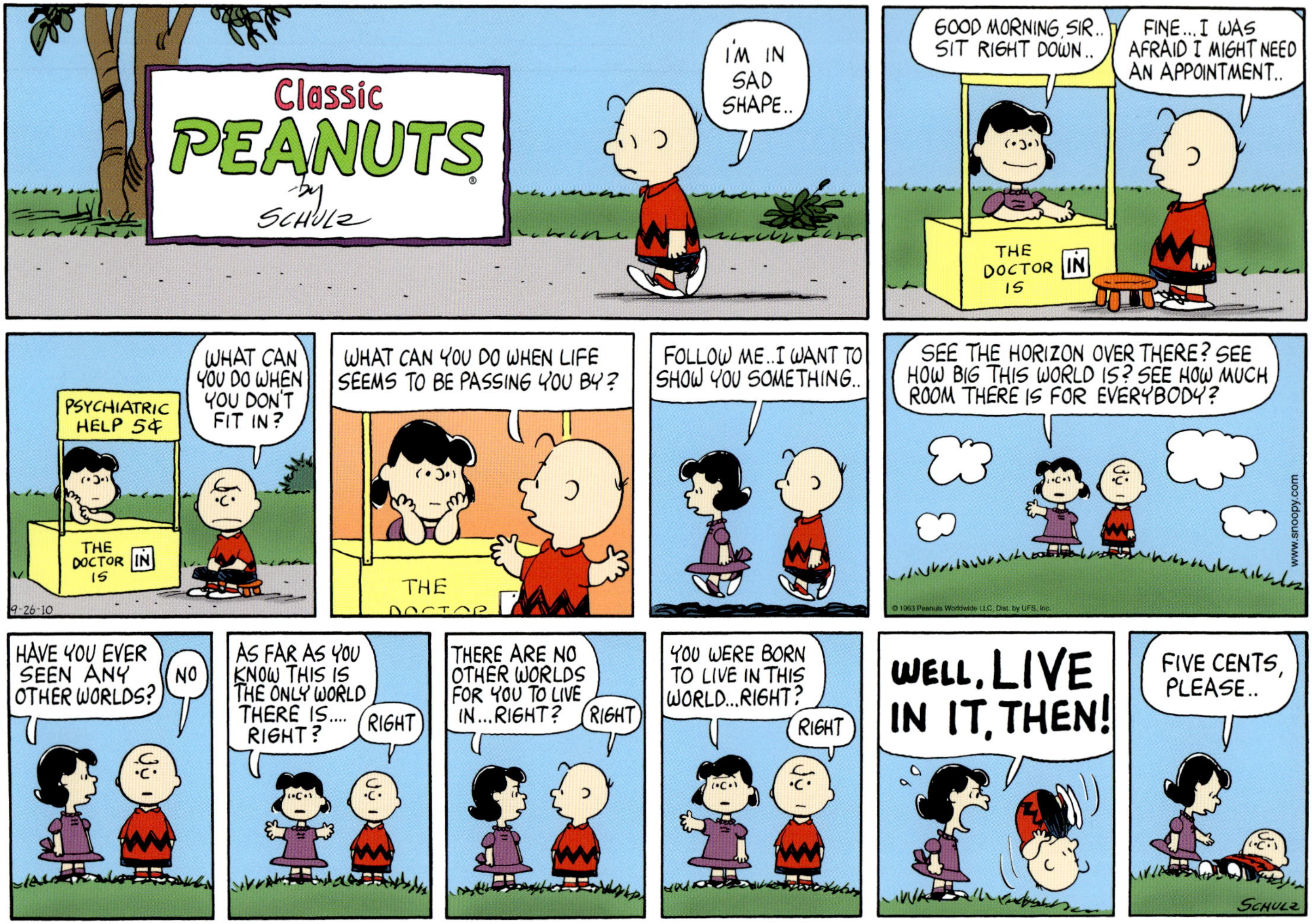
Classic
PEANUTS
by SCHULZ
I'M IN SAD SHAPE..
GOOD MORNING, SIR.. SIT RIGHT DOWN..
FINE... I WAS AFRAID I MIGHT NEED AN APPOINTMENT..
THE DOCTOR IS IN
PSYCHIATRIC HELP 5¢
WHAT CAN YOU DO WHEN YOU DON'T FIT IN?
THE DOCTOR IS IN
9-26-10
WHAT CAN YOU DO WHEN LIFE SEEMS TO BE PASSING YOU BY?
THE
FOLLOW ME..I WANT TO SHOW YOU SOMETHING..
SEE THE HORIZON OVER THERE? SEE HOW BIG THIS WORLD IS? SEE HOW MUCH ROOM THERE IS FOR EVERYBODY?
www.snoopy.com
© 1963 Peanuts Worldwide LLC, Dist. by UFS, Inc.
HAVE YOU EVER SEEN ANY OTHER WORLDS?
NO
AS FAR AS YOU KNOW THIS IS THE ONLY WORLD THERE IS.... RIGHT?
RIGHT
THERE ARE NO OTHER WORLDS FOR YOU TO LIVE IN... RIGHT?
RIGHT
YOU WERE BORN TO LIVE IN THIS WORLD... RIGHT?
RIGHT
WELL, LIVE IN IT, THEN!
FIVE CENTS, PLEASE..
SCHULZ

NOTES

September 2013

S	M	T	W	T	F	S
1	2	3	4	5	6	7
8	9	10	11	12	13	14
15	16	17	18	19	20	21
22	23	24	25	26	27	28
29	30					

SEPTEMBER

16 MONDAY

17 TUESDAY

18 WEDNESDAY

19 THURSDAY

20 FRIDAY

21 SATURDAY

U.N. International Day of Peace

22 SUNDAY

NOTES

September 2013

S	M	T	W	T	F	S
1	2	3	4	5	6	7
8	9	10	11	12	13	14
15	16	17	18	19	20	21
22	23	24	25	26	27	28
29	30					

SEPTEMBER

23 MONDAY

24 TUESDAY

25 WEDNESDAY

26 THURSDAY

27 FRIDAY

28 SATURDAY

29 SUNDAY

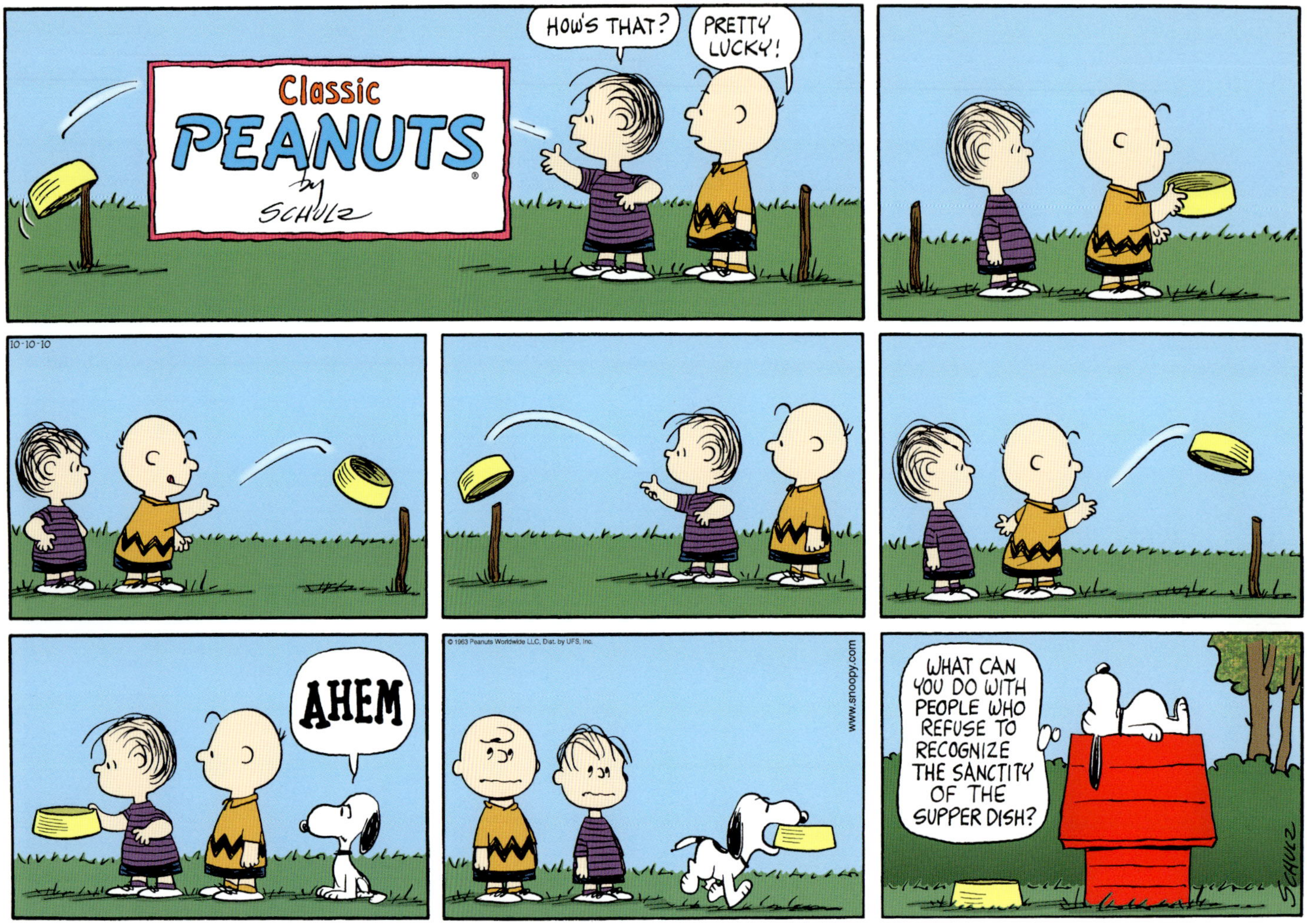
Classic
PEANUTS
by SCHULZ
HOW'S THAT?
PRETTY LUCKY!
10-10-10
AHEM
© 1963 Peanuts Worldwide LLC, Dist. by UFS, Inc.
www.snoopy.com
WHAT CAN YOU DO WITH PEOPLE WHO REFUSE TO RECOGNIZE THE SANCTITY OF THE SUPPER DISH?
SCHULZ

NOTES

September 2013

S	M	T	W	T	F	S
1	2	3	4	5	6	7
8	9	10	11	12	13	14
15	16	17	18	19	20	21
22	23	24	25	26	27	28
29	30					

October 2013

S	M	T	W	T	F	S
		1	2	3	4	5
6	7	8	9	10	11	12
13	14	15	16	17	18	19
20	21	22	23	24	25	26
27	28	29	30	31		

SEPTEMBER–OCTOBER

30 MONDAY

Queen's Birthday (Australia—WA)

1 TUESDAY

2 WEDNESDAY

3 THURSDAY

4 FRIDAY

5 SATURDAY

6 SUNDAY

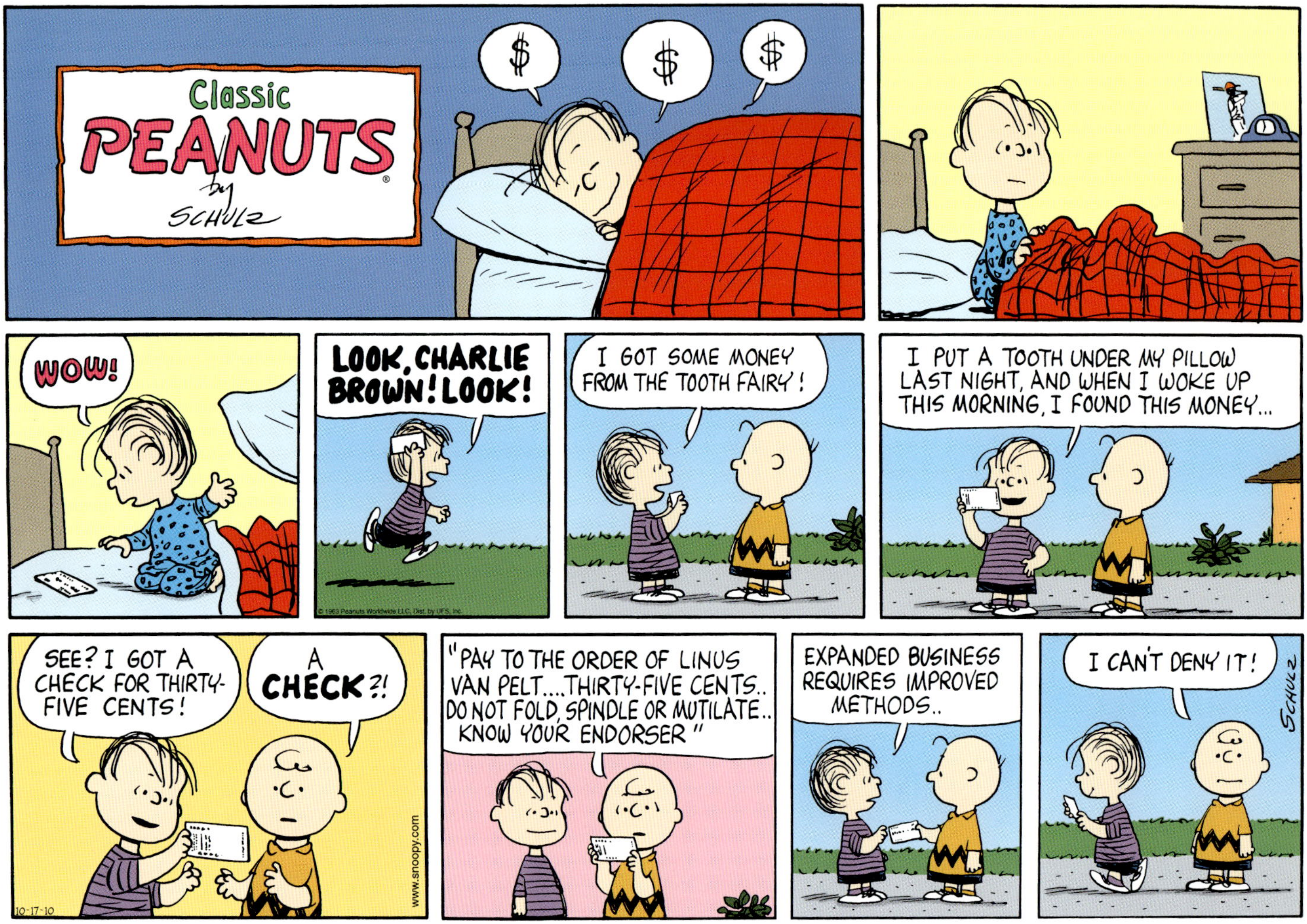
Classic
PEANUTS
by
SCHULZ
$
$
$
WOW!
LOOK, CHARLIE BROWN! LOOK!
© 1963 Peanuts Worldwide LLC, Dist. by UFS, Inc.
I GOT SOME MONEY FROM THE TOOTH FAIRY!
I PUT A TOOTH UNDER MY PILLOW LAST NIGHT, AND WHEN I WOKE UP THIS MORNING, I FOUND THIS MONEY...
SEE? I GOT A CHECK FOR THIRTY-FIVE CENTS!
A CHECK?!
10-17-10
www.snoopy.com
"PAY TO THE ORDER OF LINUS VAN PELT....THIRTY-FIVE CENTS.. DO NOT FOLD, SPINDLE OR MUTILATE.. KNOW YOUR ENDORSER"
EXPANDED BUSINESS REQUIRES IMPROVED METHODS..
I CAN'T DENY IT!
SCHULZ

NOTES

October 2013

S	M	T	W	T	F	S
		1	2	3	4	5
6	7	8	9	10	11	12
13	14	15	16	17	18	19
20	21	22	23	24	25	26
27	28	29	30	31		

OCTOBER

7 MONDAY

Labour Day (Australia—ACT, SA, NSW)

8 TUESDAY

9 WEDNESDAY

10 THURSDAY

11 FRIDAY

12 SATURDAY

13 SUNDAY

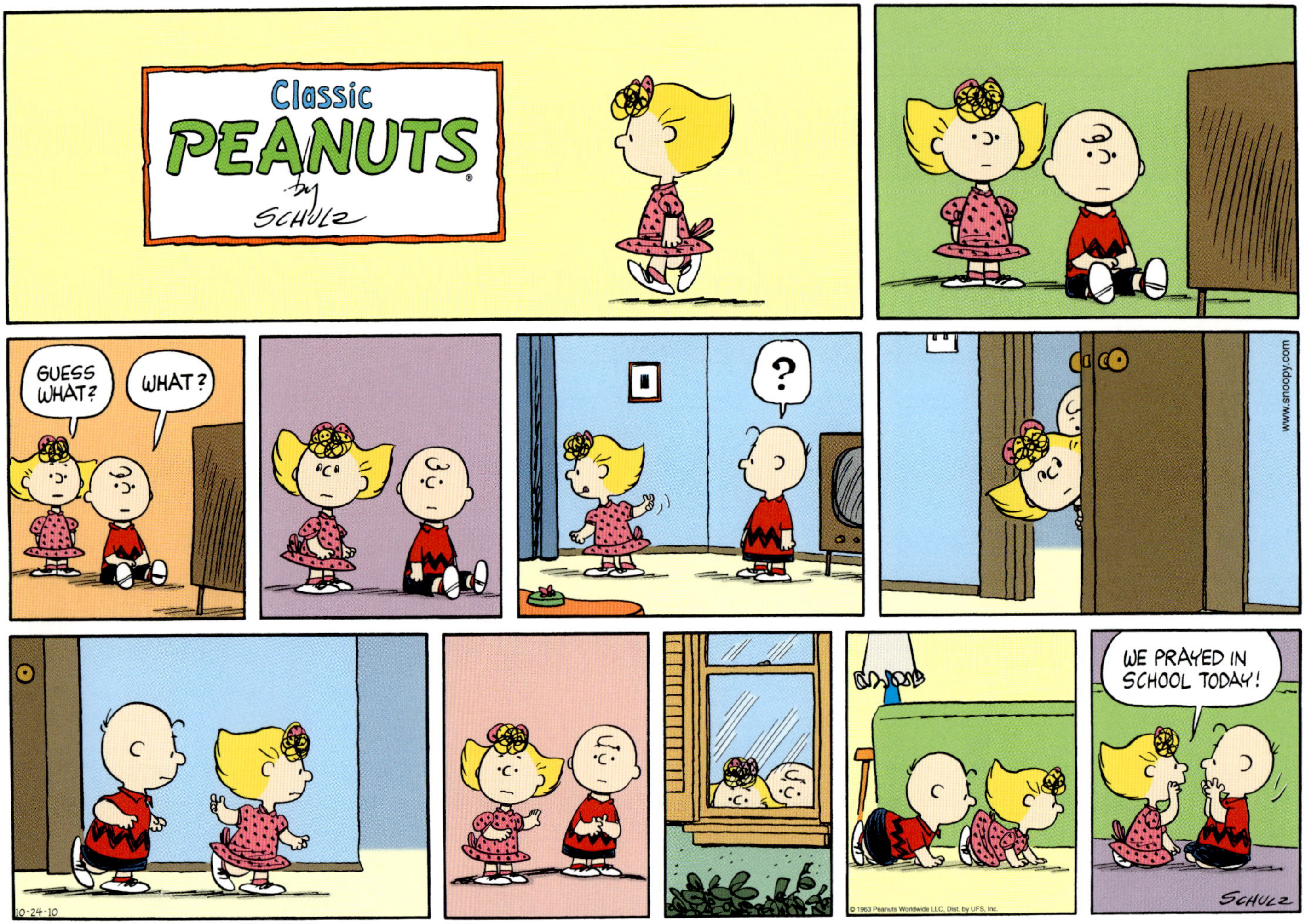
Classic
PEANUTS
by SCHULZ
GUESS WHAT?
WHAT?
?
www.snoopy.com
10-24-10
© 1963 Peanuts Worldwide LLC, Dist. by UFS, Inc.
WE PRAYED IN SCHOOL TODAY!
SCHULZ

NOTES

October 2013

S	M	T	W	T	F	S
		1	2	3	4	5
6	7	8	9	10	11	12
13	14	15	16	17	18	19
20	21	22	23	24	25	26
27	28	29	30	31		

OCTOBER

14 MONDAY

Columbus Day (USA)

Thanksgiving (Canada)

15 TUESDAY

Eid al-Adha

16 WEDNESDAY

17 THURSDAY

18 FRIDAY

19 SATURDAY

20 SUNDAY

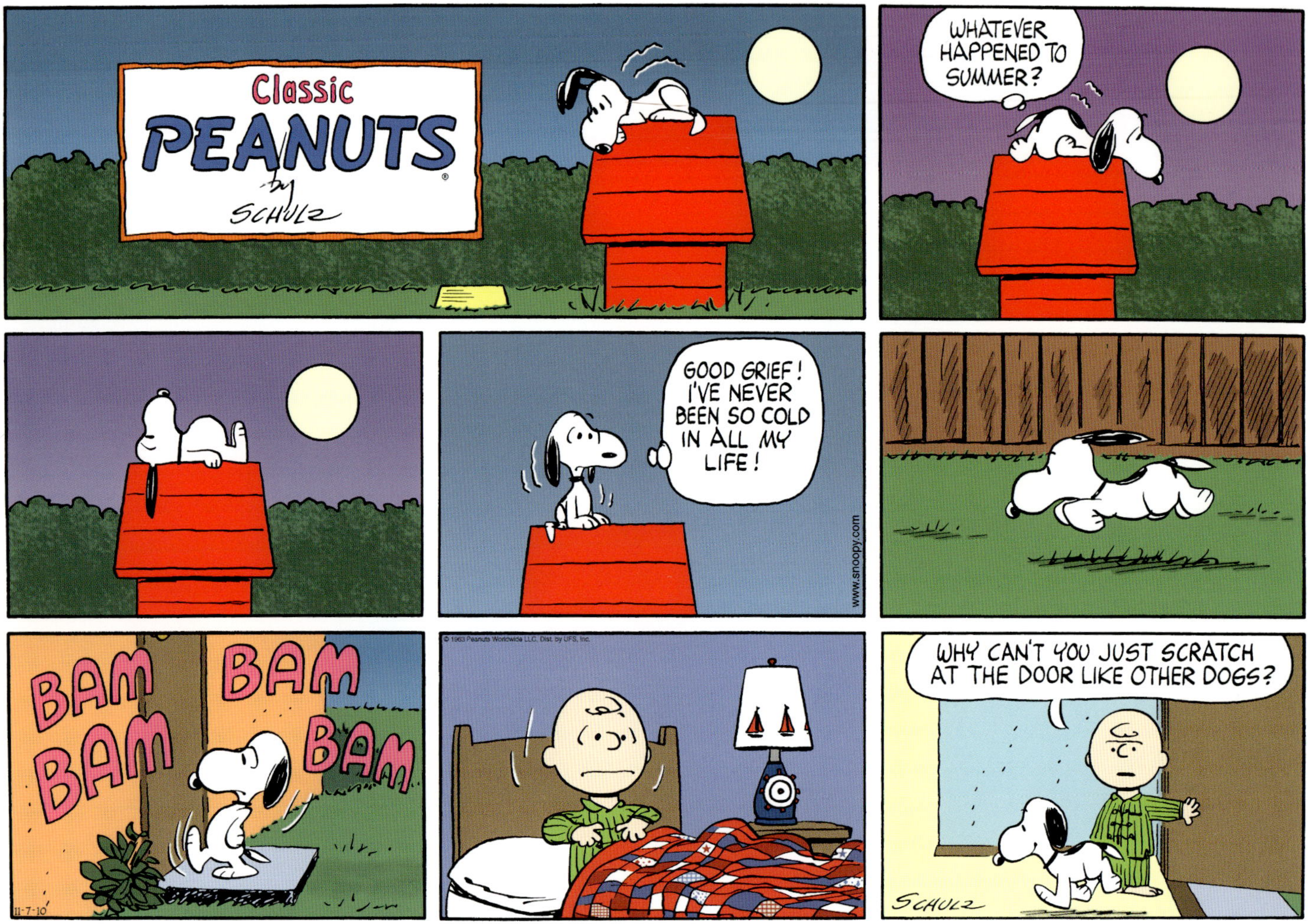
Classic
PEANUTS
by SCHULZ
WHATEVER HAPPENED TO SUMMER?
GOOD GRIEF! I'VE NEVER BEEN SO COLD IN ALL MY LIFE!
www.snoopy.com
BAM BAM
BAM BAM
© 1963 Peanuts Worldwide LLC. Dist. by UFS, Inc.
WHY CAN'T YOU JUST SCRATCH AT THE DOOR LIKE OTHER DOGS?
SCHULZ

NOTES

October 2013

S	M	T	W	T	F	S
		1	2	3	4	5
6	7	8	9	10	11	12
13	14	15	16	17	18	19
20	21	22	23	24	25	26
27	28	29	30	31		

OCTOBER

21 MONDAY

22 TUESDAY

23 WEDNESDAY

24 THURSDAY

United Nations Day

25 FRIDAY

26 SATURDAY

27 SUNDAY

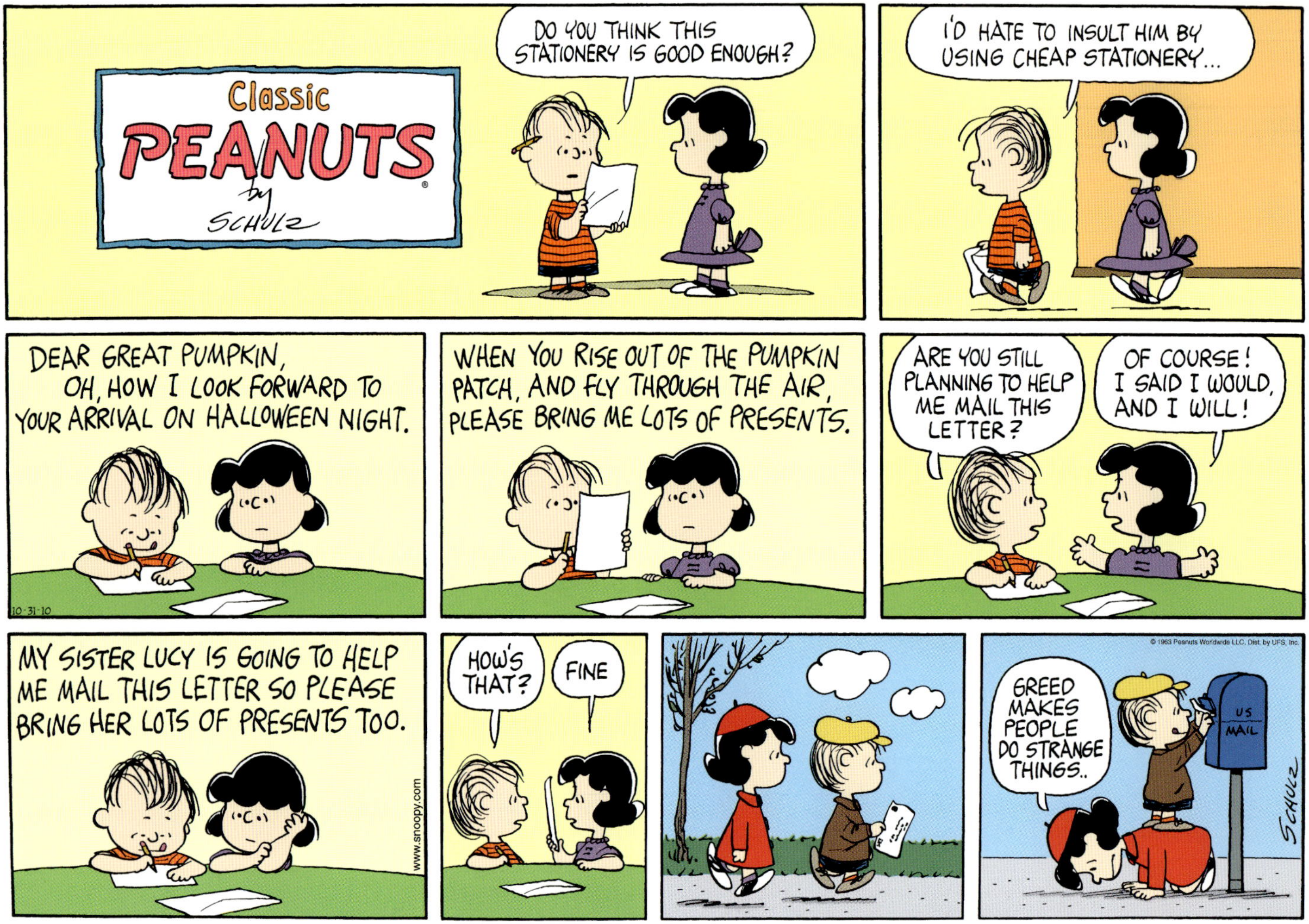
Classic
PEANUTS
by SCHULZ
DO YOU THINK THIS STATIONERY IS GOOD ENOUGH?
I'D HATE TO INSULT HIM BY USING CHEAP STATIONERY...
DEAR GREAT PUMPKIN,
OH, HOW I LOOK FORWARD TO YOUR ARRIVAL ON HALLOWEEN NIGHT.
10-31-10
WHEN YOU RISE OUT OF THE PUMPKIN PATCH, AND FLY THROUGH THE AIR, PLEASE BRING ME LOTS OF PRESENTS.
ARE YOU STILL PLANNING TO HELP ME MAIL THIS LETTER?
OF COURSE! I SAID I WOULD, AND I WILL!
MY SISTER LUCY IS GOING TO HELP ME MAIL THIS LETTER SO PLEASE BRING HER LOTS OF PRESENTS TOO.
www.snoopy.com
HOW'S THAT?
FINE
© 1963 Peanuts Worldwide LLC, Dist. by UFS, Inc.
GREED MAKES PEOPLE DO STRANGE THINGS..
US MAIL
SCHULZ

NOTES

October 2013

S	M	T	W	T	F	S
		1	2	3	4	5
6	7	8	9	10	11	12
13	14	15	16	17	18	19
20	21	22	23	24	25	26
27	28	29	30	31		

November 2013

S	M	T	W	T	F	S
					1	2
3	4	5	6	7	8	9
10	11	12	13	14	15	16
17	18	19	20	21	22	23
24	25	26	27	28	29	30

OCTOBER–NOVEMBER

28 MONDAY

Labour Day (NZ)

Bank Holiday (Ireland)

29 TUESDAY

30 WEDNESDAY

31 THURSDAY

Halloween

1 FRIDAY

2 SATURDAY

3 SUNDAY

Classic PEANUTS by SCHULZ
RATS!
I HATE SUNDAY AFTERNOONS!
THERE'S NOTHING TO DO..
WHY DON'T YOU GO JUMP IN SOME LEAVES?
THAT'S NOT A NICE THING TO SAY!
NO, I MEAN IT... THIS IS THE TIME OF YEAR FOR IT..
REALLY?
OF COURSE! IT'S FUN... IT'S EVEN TRADITIONAL... KIDS HAVE BEEN DOING IT SINCE THE WORLD BEGAN..
JUST GET YOURSELF A BIG PILE OF LEAVES...THEN BACK OFF, TAKE A GOOD RUN AND JUMP RIGHT IN!
IT SOUNDS GREAT..
© 1963 Peanuts Worldwide LLC, Dist. by UFS, Inc.
www.snoopy.com
WHERE DOES ONE GO TO PURCHASE A PILE OF LEAVES?
SCHULZ

NOTES

November 2013

S	M	T	W	T	F	S
					1	2
3	4	5	6	7	8	9
10	11	12	13	14	15	16
17	18	19	20	21	22	23
24	25	26	27	28	29	30

NOVEMBER

4 MONDAY

5 TUESDAY

Election Day (USA)

6 WEDNESDAY

7 THURSDAY

8 FRIDAY

9 SATURDAY

10 SUNDAY

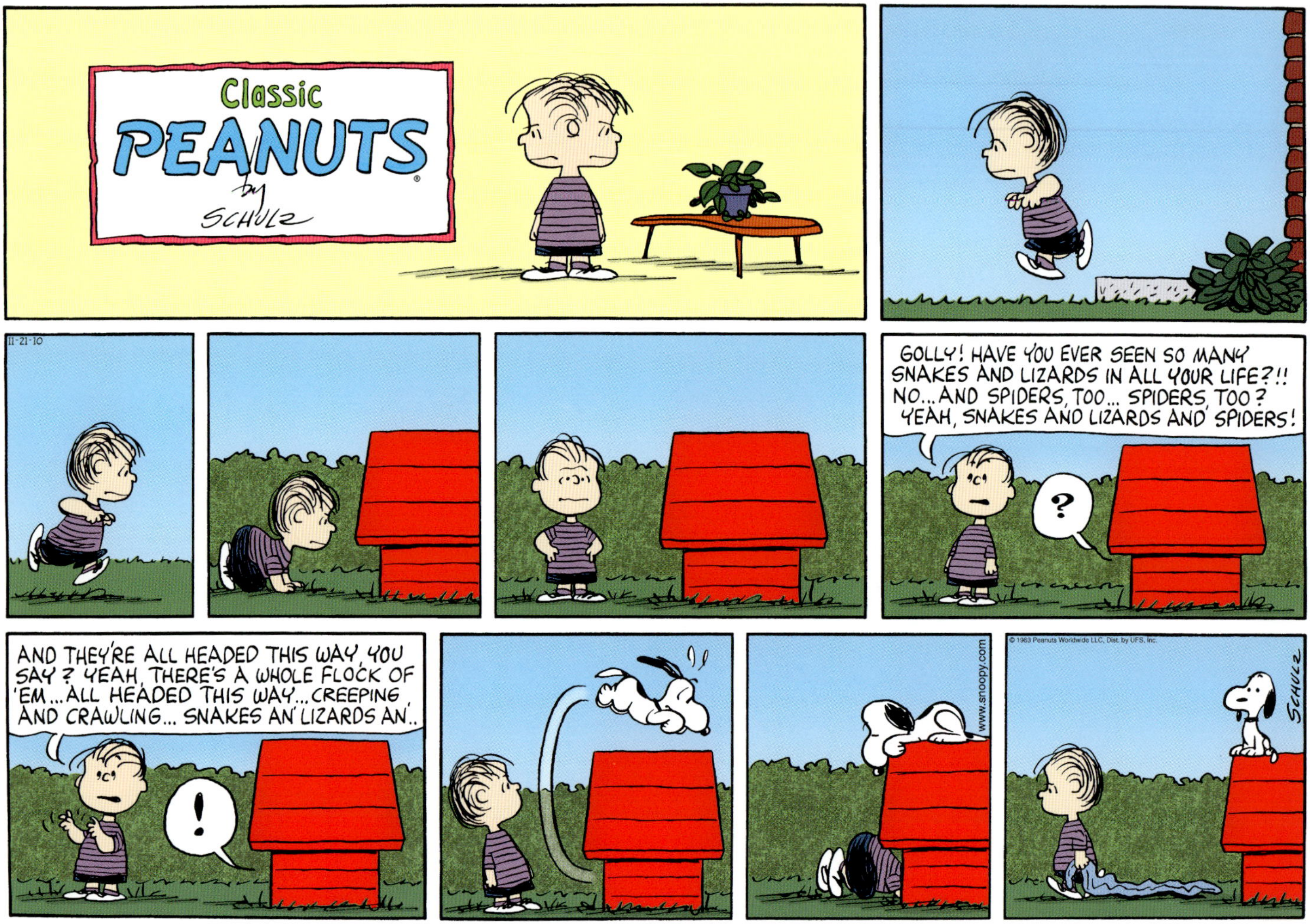
Classic
PEANUTS
by SCHULZ
11-21-10
GOLLY! HAVE YOU EVER SEEN SO MANY SNAKES AND LIZARDS IN ALL YOUR LIFE?!! NO...AND SPIDERS, TOO... SPIDERS, TOO? YEAH, SNAKES AND LIZARDS AND SPIDERS!
?
AND THEY'RE ALL HEADED THIS WAY, YOU SAY? YEAH, THERE'S A WHOLE FLOCK OF 'EM...ALL HEADED THIS WAY...CREEPING AND CRAWLING... SNAKES AN' LIZARDS AN'..
!
www.snoopy.com
© 1963 Peanuts Worldwide LLC, Dist. by UFS, Inc.
SCHULZ

NOTES

November 2013

S	M	T	W	T	F	S
					1	2
3	4	5	6	7	8	9
10	11	12	13	14	15	16
17	18	19	20	21	22	23
24	25	26	27	28	29	30

NOVEMBER

11 MONDAY

Veterans' Day (USA)

Remembrance Day (Canada, Ireland, UK)

12 TUESDAY

13 WEDNESDAY

14 THURSDAY

15 FRIDAY

16 SATURDAY

17 SUNDAY

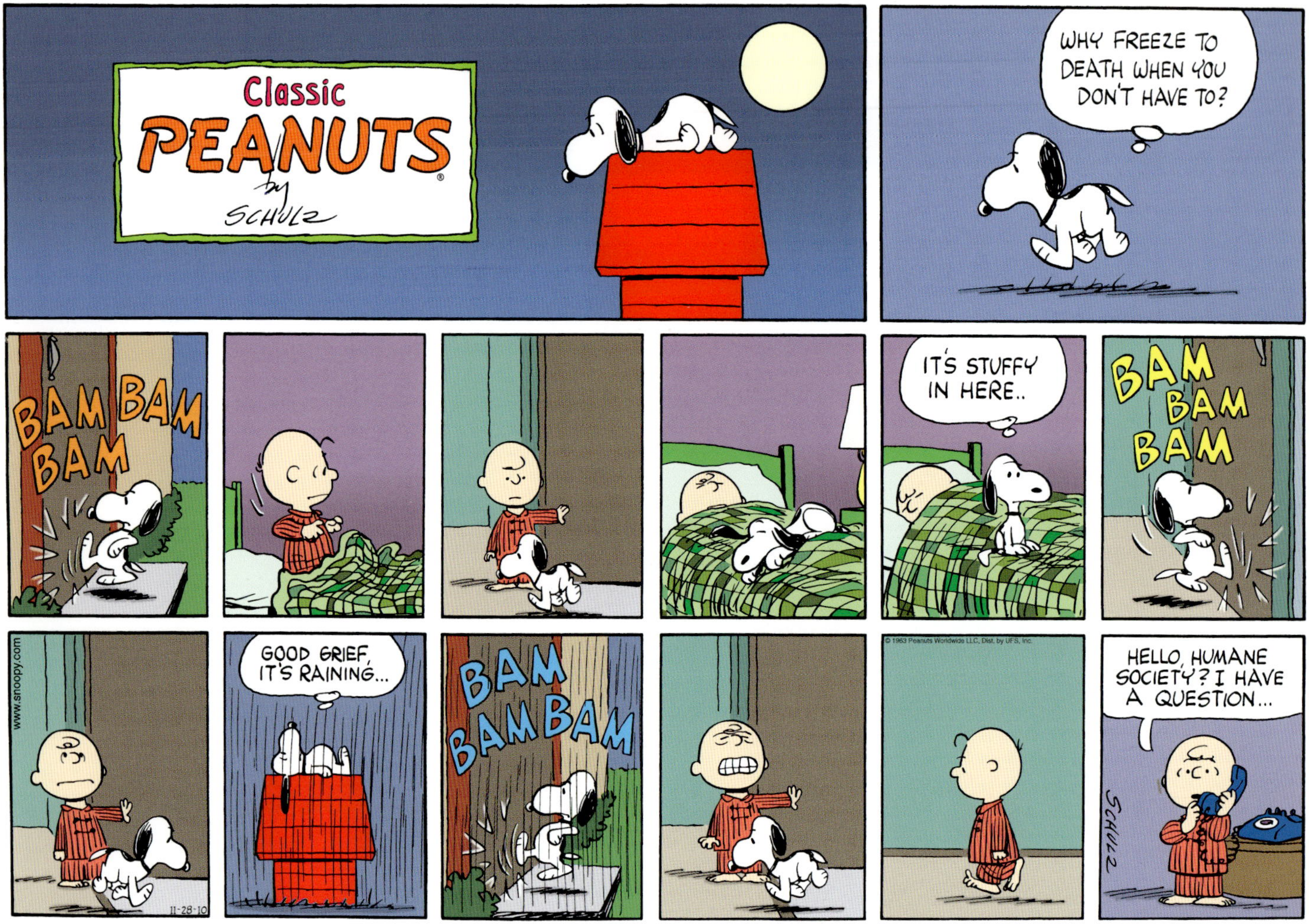

Classic
PEANUTS
by SCHULZ
WHY FREEZE TO DEATH WHEN YOU DON'T HAVE TO?
BAM BAM BAM BAM
IT'S STUFFY IN HERE..
BAM BAM BAM
www.snoopy.com
11-28-10
GOOD GRIEF, IT'S RAINING...
BAM BAM BAM
© 1963 Peanuts Worldwide LLC, Dist. by UFS, Inc.
SCHULZ
HELLO, HUMANE SOCIETY? I HAVE A QUESTION...

NOTES

November 2013

S	M	T	W	T	F	S
					1	2
3	4	5	6	7	8	9
10	11	12	13	14	15	16
17	18	19	20	21	22	23
24	25	26	27	28	29	30

NOVEMBER

18 MONDAY

19 TUESDAY

20 WEDNESDAY

21 THURSDAY

22 FRIDAY

23 SATURDAY

24 SUNDAY

Classic
PEANUTS
by SCHULZ
BOY, I'LL BET IT WAS TEN-BELOW LAST NIGHT..
SNOW!
HEY, LINUS..C'MON OUTSIDE...IT SNOWED LAST NIGHT!
?
?
www.snoopy.com
I DON'T SEE ANY SNOW...
© 1963 Peanuts Worldwide LLC
NOT DOWN HERE..
12-5-10
UP ON THE PEAK!
SCHULZ

NOTES

November 2013						
S	M	T	W	T	F	S
					1	2
3	4	5	6	7	8	9
10	11	12	13	14	15	16
17	18	19	20	21	22	23
24	25	26	27	28	29	30

December 2013						
S	M	T	W	T	F	S
1	2	3	4	5	6	7
8	9	10	11	12	13	14
15	16	17	18	19	20	21
22	23	24	25	26	27	28
29	30	31				

NOVEMBER–DECEMBER

25 MONDAY

26 TUESDAY

27 WEDNESDAY

28 THURSDAY

Thanksgiving (USA)

*Hanukkah**

29 FRIDAY

30 SATURDAY

St. Andrew's Day (UK)

1 SUNDAY

**Begins at sundown the previous day*

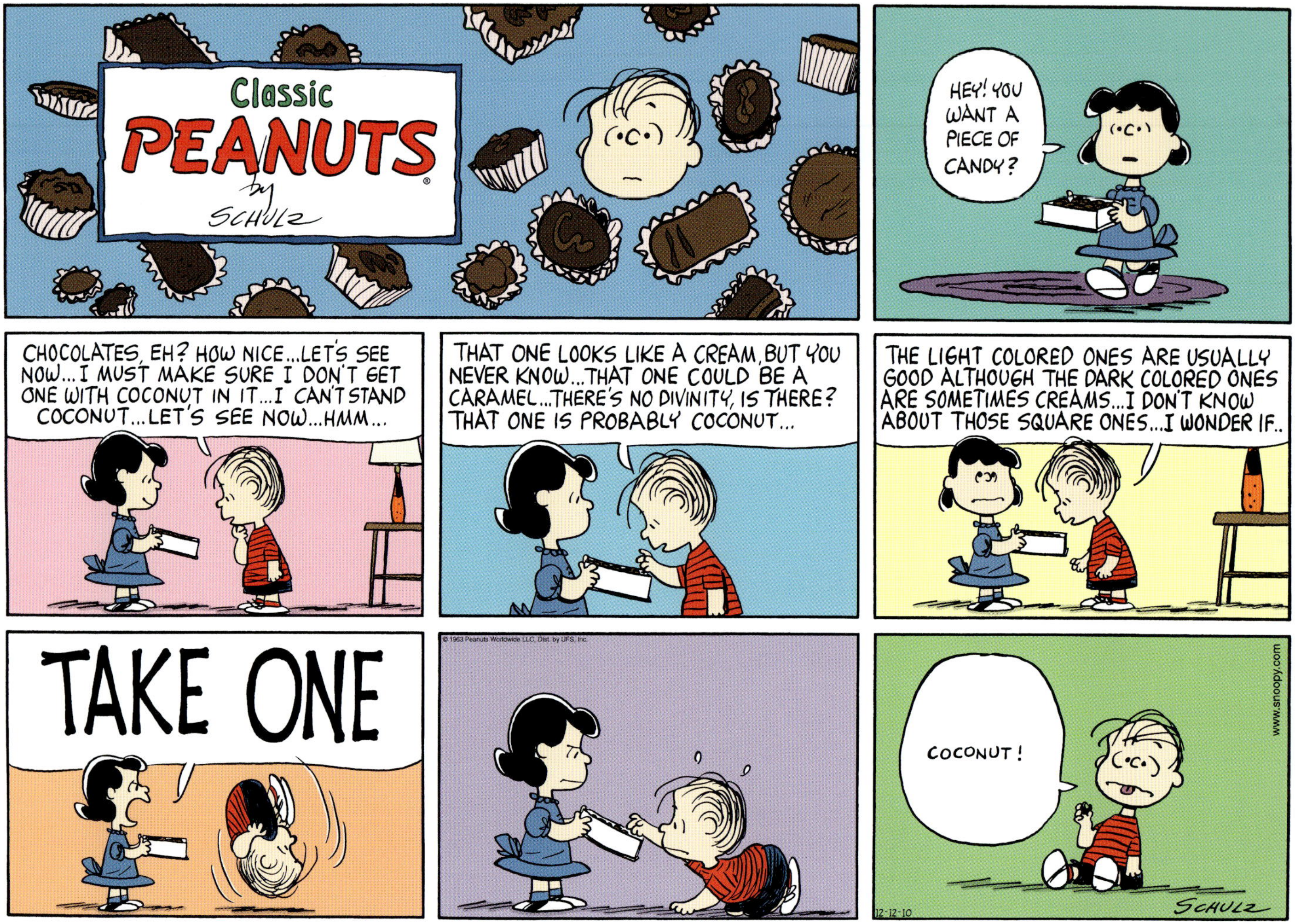
Classic
PEANUTS
by SCHULZ
HEY! YOU WANT A PIECE OF CANDY?
CHOCOLATES, EH? HOW NICE...LET'S SEE NOW...I MUST MAKE SURE I DON'T GET ONE WITH COCONUT IN IT...I CAN'T STAND COCONUT...LET'S SEE NOW...HMM...
THAT ONE LOOKS LIKE A CREAM, BUT YOU NEVER KNOW...THAT ONE COULD BE A CARAMEL...THERE'S NO DIVINITY, IS THERE? THAT ONE IS PROBABLY COCONUT...
THE LIGHT COLORED ONES ARE USUALLY GOOD ALTHOUGH THE DARK COLORED ONES ARE SOMETIMES CREAMS...I DON'T KNOW ABOUT THOSE SQUARE ONES...I WONDER IF..
TAKE ONE
© 1963 Peanuts Worldwide LLC, Dist. by UFS, Inc.
COCONUT!
www.snoopy.com
12-12-10
SCHULZ

NOTES

December 2013

S	M	T	W	T	F	S
1	2	3	4	5	6	7
8	9	10	11	12	13	14
15	16	17	18	19	20	21
22	23	24	25	26	27	28
29	30	31				

DECEMBER

2 MONDAY

St. Andrew's Day (observed) (UK—Scotland)

3 TUESDAY

4 WEDNESDAY

5 THURSDAY

Hanukkah ends

6 FRIDAY

7 SATURDAY

8 SUNDAY

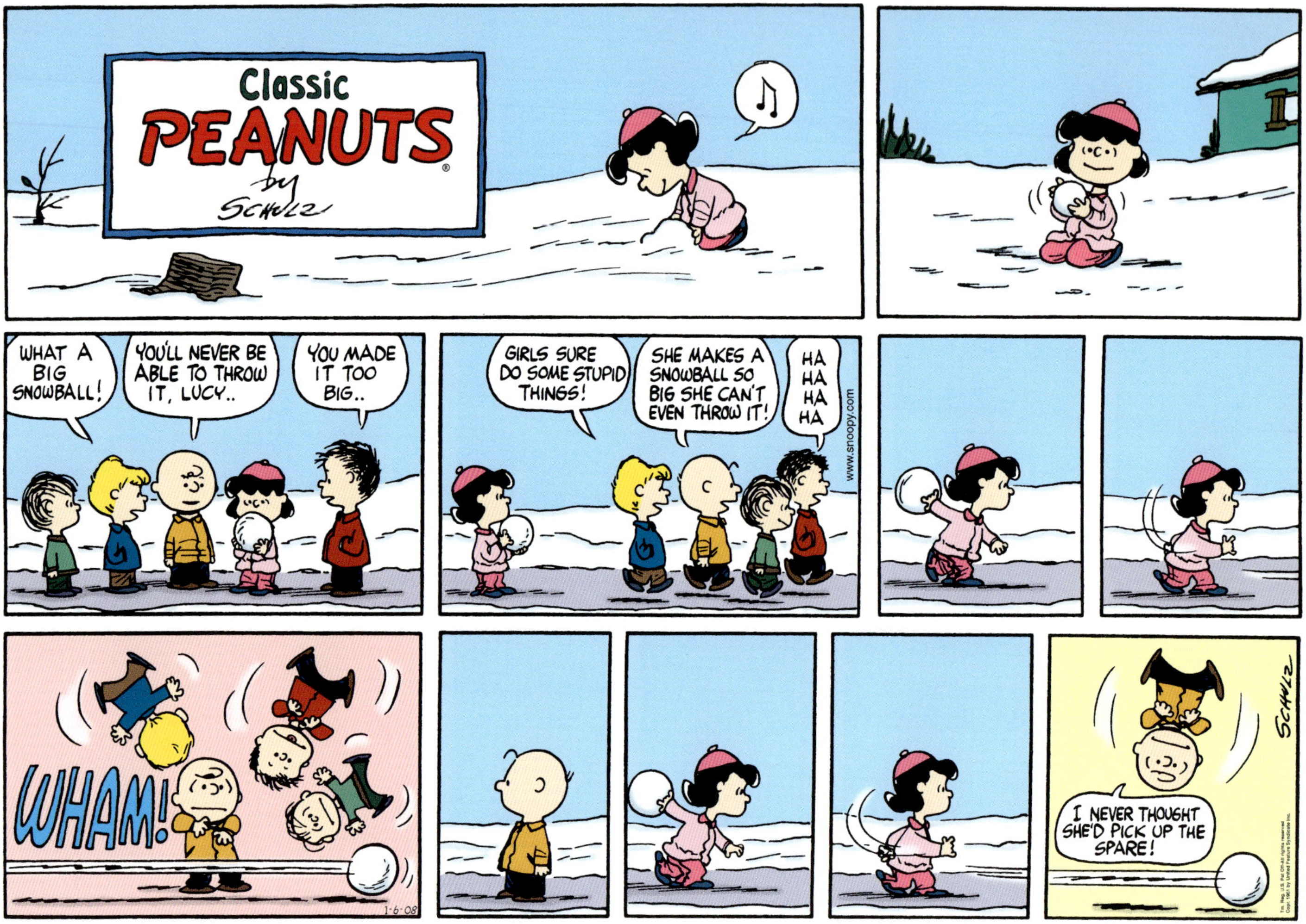

Classic PEANUTS by SCHULZ
♪
WHAT A BIG SNOWBALL!
YOU'LL NEVER BE ABLE TO THROW IT, LUCY..
YOU MADE IT TOO BIG..
GIRLS SURE DO SOME STUPID THINGS!
SHE MAKES A SNOWBALL SO BIG SHE CAN'T EVEN THROW IT!
HA HA HA HA
www.snoopy.com
WHAM!
1-6-08
SCHULZ
I NEVER THOUGHT SHE'D PICK UP THE SPARE!
Tm. Reg. U.S. Pat Off-All rights reserved
Copr. 1961 by United Feature Syndicate Inc.

NOTES

December 2013

S	M	T	W	T	F	S
1	2	3	4	5	6	7
8	9	10	11	12	13	14
15	16	17	18	19	20	21
22	23	24	25	26	27	28
29	30	31				

DECEMBER

9 MONDAY

10 TUESDAY

Human Rights Day

11 WEDNESDAY

12 THURSDAY

13 FRIDAY

14 SATURDAY

15 SUNDAY

Classic
PEANUTS
by SCHULZ
WHOP!
HA! PRETTY GOOD SHOT, EH, LINUS?
DON'T YOU WISH YOU COULD THROW A SNOWBALL THAT FAR?
www.snoopy.com
WHANG!
1-27-08
FOR THE FIRST TIME IN MY LIFE I HAVE A SLIGHT IDEA OF HOW GOLIATH MUST HAVE FELT!
SCHULZ

NOTES

December 2013

S	M	T	W	T	F	S
1	2	3	4	5	6	7
8	9	10	11	12	13	14
15	16	17	18	19	20	21
22	23	24	25	26	27	28
29	30	31				

DECEMBER

16 MONDAY

17 TUESDAY

18 WEDNESDAY

19 THURSDAY

20 FRIDAY

21 SATURDAY

22 SUNDAY

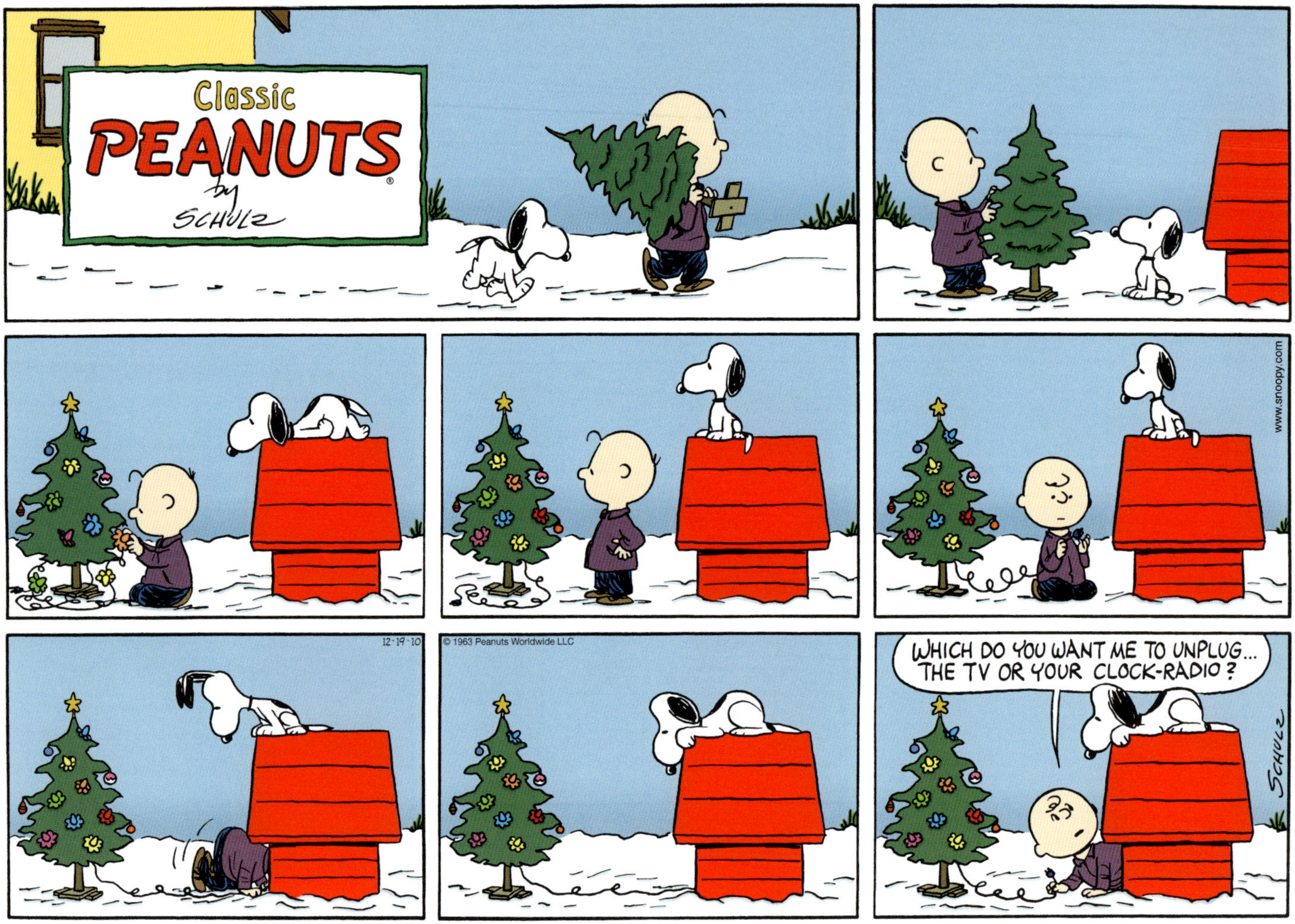
Classic
PEANUTS
by SCHULZ
www.snoopy.com
12-19-10
© 1963 Peanuts Worldwide LLC
WHICH DO YOU WANT ME TO UNPLUG... THE TV OR YOUR CLOCK-RADIO?
SCHULZ

NOTES

December 2013

S	M	T	W	T	F	S
1	2	3	4	5	6	7
8	9	10	11	12	13	14
15	16	17	18	19	20	21
22	23	24	25	26	27	28
29	30	31				

DECEMBER

23 MONDAY

24 TUESDAY

Christmas Eve

25 WEDNESDAY

Christmas Day

26 THURSDAY

Kwanzaa begins (USA)

Boxing Day
(Canada, NZ, UK, Australia—except SA)

St. Stephen's Day (Ireland)

Proclamation Day (Australia—SA)

27 FRIDAY

28 SATURDAY

29 SUNDAY

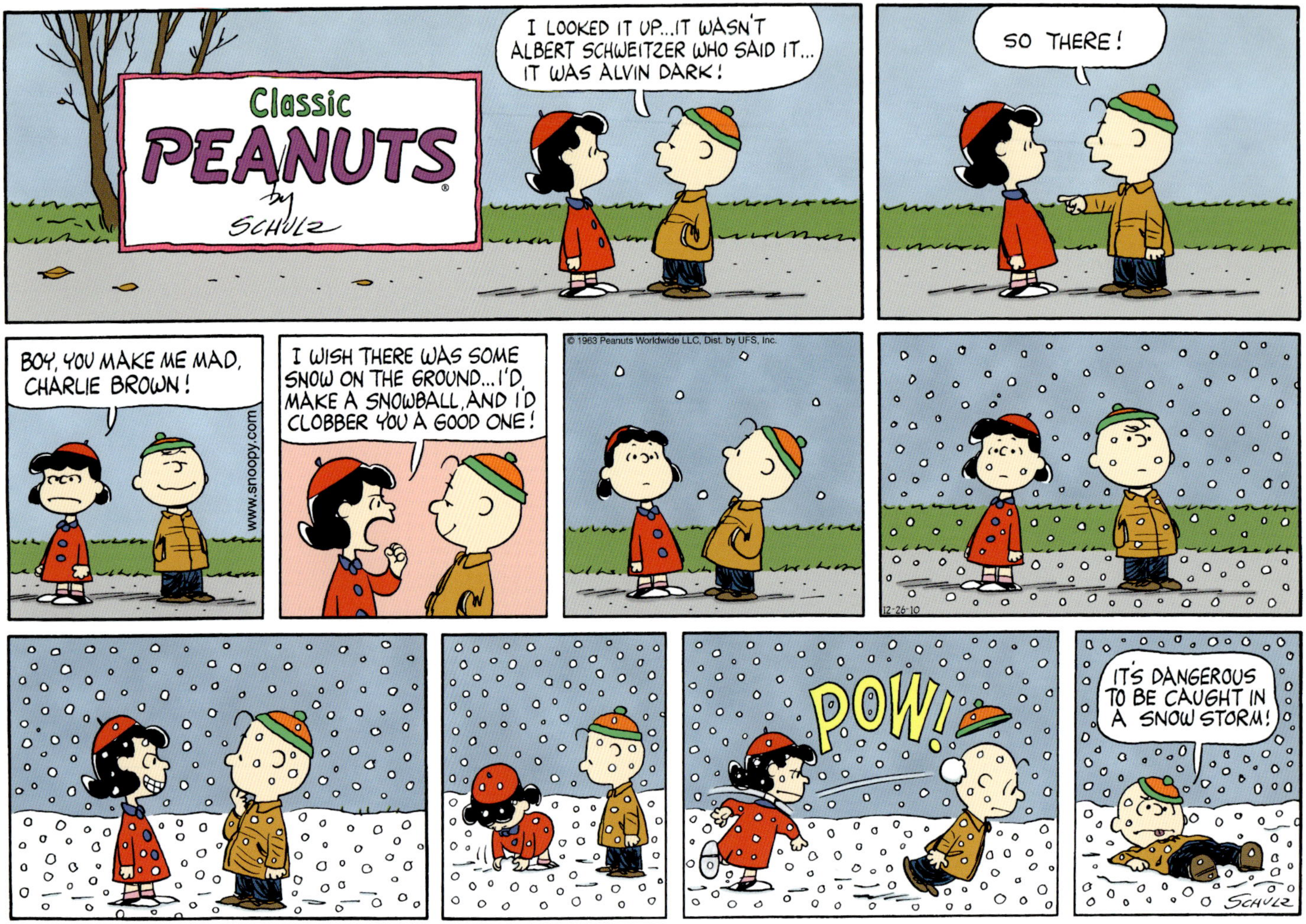

Classic
PEANUTS
by SCHULZ
I LOOKED IT UP...IT WASN'T ALBERT SCHWEITZER WHO SAID IT... IT WAS ALVIN DARK!
SO THERE!
BOY, YOU MAKE ME MAD, CHARLIE BROWN!
www.snoopy.com
I WISH THERE WAS SOME SNOW ON THE GROUND...I'D MAKE A SNOWBALL, AND I'D CLOBBER YOU A GOOD ONE!
© 1963 Peanuts Worldwide LLC, Dist. by UFS, Inc.
12-26-10
POW!
IT'S DANGEROUS TO BE CAUGHT IN A SNOW STORM!
SCHULZ

NOTES

December 2013

S	M	T	W	T	F	S
1	2	3	4	5	6	7
8	9	10	11	12	13	14
15	16	17	18	19	20	21
22	23	24	25	26	27	28
29	30	31				

January 2014

S	M	T	W	T	F	S
			1	2	3	4
5	6	7	8	9	10	11
12	13	14	15	16	17	18
19	20	21	22	23	24	25
26	27	28	29	30	31	

DECEMBER 2013–JANUARY 2014

30 MONDAY

31 TUESDAY

1 WEDNESDAY

New Year's Day

Kwanzaa ends (USA)

2 THURSDAY

Bank Holiday (UK—Scotland)

3 FRIDAY

4 SATURDAY

5 SUNDAY

2014

JANUARY

FEBRUARY

MARCH

APRIL

MAY

JUNE

JULY

AUGUST

SEPTEMBER

OCTOBER

NOVEMBER

DECEMBER

2012

JANUARY

S	M	T	W	T	F	S
1	2	3	4	5	6	7
8	9	10	11	12	13	14
15	16	17	18	19	20	21
22	23	24	25	26	27	28
29	30	31				

FEBRUARY

S	M	T	W	T	F	S
			1	2	3	4
5	6	7	8	9	10	11
12	13	14	15	16	17	18
19	20	21	22	23	24	25
26	27	28	29			

MARCH

S	M	T	W	T	F	S
				1	2	3
4	5	6	7	8	9	10
11	12	13	14	15	16	17
18	19	20	21	22	23	24
25	26	27	28	29	30	31

APRIL

S	M	T	W	T	F	S
1	2	3	4	5	6	7
8	9	10	11	12	13	14
15	16	17	18	19	20	21
22	23	24	25	26	27	28
29	30					

MAY

S	M	T	W	T	F	S
		1	2	3	4	5
6	7	8	9	10	11	12
13	14	15	16	17	18	19
20	21	22	23	24	25	26
27	28	29	30	31		

JUNE

S	M	T	W	T	F	S
					1	2
3	4	5	6	7	8	9
10	11	12	13	14	15	16
17	18	19	20	21	22	23
24	25	26	27	28	29	30

JULY

S	M	T	W	T	F	S
1	2	3	4	5	6	7
8	9	10	11	12	13	14
15	16	17	18	19	20	21
22	23	24	25	26	27	28
29	30	31				

AUGUST

S	M	T	W	T	F	S
			1	2	3	4
5	6	7	8	9	10	11
12	13	14	15	16	17	18
19	20	21	22	23	24	25
26	27	28	29	30	31	

SEPTEMBER

S	M	T	W	T	F	S
						1
2	3	4	5	6	7	8
9	10	11	12	13	14	15
16	17	18	19	20	21	22
23	24	25	26	27	28	29
30						

OCTOBER

S	M	T	W	T	F	S
	1	2	3	4	5	6
7	8	9	10	11	12	13
14	15	16	17	18	19	20
21	22	23	24	25	26	27
28	29	30	31			

NOVEMBER

S	M	T	W	T	F	S
				1	2	3
4	5	6	7	8	9	10
11	12	13	14	15	16	17
18	19	20	21	22	23	24
25	26	27	28	29	30	

DECEMBER

S	M	T	W	T	F	S
						1
2	3	4	5	6	7	8
9	10	11	12	13	14	15
16	17	18	19	20	21	22
23	24	25	26	27	28	29
30	31					

2014

JANUARY

S	M	T	W	T	F	S
			1	2	3	4
5	6	7	8	9	10	11
12	13	14	15	16	17	18
19	20	21	22	23	24	25
26	27	28	29	30	31	

FEBRUARY

S	M	T	W	T	F	S
						1
2	3	4	5	6	7	8
9	10	11	12	13	14	15
16	17	18	19	20	21	22
23	24	25	26	27	28	

MARCH

S	M	T	W	T	F	S
						1
2	3	4	5	6	7	8
9	10	11	12	13	14	15
16	17	18	19	20	21	22
23	24	25	26	27	28	29
30	31					

APRIL

S	M	T	W	T	F	S
		1	2	3	4	5
6	7	8	9	10	11	12
13	14	15	16	17	18	19
20	21	22	23	24	25	26
27	28	29	30			

MAY

S	M	T	W	T	F	S
				1	2	3
4	5	6	7	8	9	10
11	12	13	14	15	16	17
18	19	20	21	22	23	24
25	26	27	28	29	30	31

JUNE

S	M	T	W	T	F	S
1	2	3	4	5	6	7
8	9	10	11	12	13	14
15	16	17	18	19	20	21
22	23	24	25	26	27	28
29	30					

JULY

S	M	T	W	T	F	S
		1	2	3	4	5
6	7	8	9	10	11	12
13	14	15	16	17	18	19
20	21	22	23	24	25	26
27	28	29	30	31		

AUGUST

S	M	T	W	T	F	S
					1	2
3	4	5	6	7	8	9
10	11	12	13	14	15	16
17	18	19	20	21	22	23
24	25	26	27	28	29	30
31						

SEPTEMBER

S	M	T	W	T	F	S
	1	2	3	4	5	6
7	8	9	10	11	12	13
14	15	16	17	18	19	20
21	22	23	24	25	26	27
28	29	30				

OCTOBER

S	M	T	W	T	F	S
			1	2	3	4
5	6	7	8	9	10	11
12	13	14	15	16	17	18
19	20	21	22	23	24	25
26	27	28	29	30	31	

NOVEMBER

S	M	T	W	T	F	S
						1
2	3	4	5	6	7	8
9	10	11	12	13	14	15
16	17	18	19	20	21	22
23	24	25	26	27	28	29
30						

DECEMBER

S	M	T	W	T	F	S
	1	2	3	4	5	6
7	8	9	10	11	12	13
14	15	16	17	18	19	20
21	22	23	24	25	26	27
28	29	30	31			